# BINGLEY

## AND SURROUNDS

# FORGOTTEN MOMENTS

## FROM HISTORY

### ALAN CATTELL

First published 2011

Published by
Overt Marketing Limited
143, Main Street, Wilsden,
Bradford, West Yorkshire
BD15 0AQ
www.overtmarketing.co.uk
www.bradfordhistory.co.uk

ISBN: 978-0-9571143-0-2

# Contents

# Preface

## Research

12 years ago I moved to Bingley knowing little about the area but interested in the wealth of history that there appeared to be locally.

During those 12 years I have spent time researching that history at Bingley, Keighley, Shipley and Bradford Libraries and at the Shipley College, Saltaire Archives. Additionally I have accessed local and national 19th Century Newspapers through the Bradford Libraries in respect particularly of Victorian sources of information.

Amongst invaluable resources have been the books written by local historians : Cudworth, Dodd, Horsfall-Turner and Speight in earlier times and Firth more recently. These have provided detail and an academic context.

As a counterpoint, more recent "histories" have tended to present pictorial, photographic presentations which are excellent on images but provide less historical information and detail.

## A Middle Road

Over the last three years I have written and published a number of local history articles about Bingley and its surrounds intended for an audience who seek a "middle road" between the detail only or photographs only approach to history.

What I seek to do within this book is to provide such a "middle road" resource which brings history visually out of the archives and into the living rooms of readers interested as I was in knowing a little about the history of the area they live in. Neither do I wish to saturate my readers with information overload.

I am a great believer in "living history" and perhaps my most valuable resources have been the people who have had relatives involved at first hand or who have themselves been involved in some of the events and have given accounts to me as a primary source of information.

This is after all their history and your history. I hope that the book provides you with a dip in, dip out reading experience which will stimulate you to visit, research or generally find out for yourself more about Bingley and Surrounds in terms of some of the "Moments" I have chosen to describe in this book. Better still if you are stimulated to find and research your own "Moments."

## Acknowledgments

In addition to the invaluable support given by my family, a number of people have been significant in my research, leading to the publication of this book.

Amongst these are my friends and neighbours Brian and Olwyn Billcliff who have been been my critical readers. Sue Caton of Bradford Libraries Local History and Julie Woodward of Shipley College, Saltaire Archives have helped enable access to materials and photographs as well as providing key advice. Roger Clarke, the Saltaire Historian has been a valued listening ear and adviser. Members of the Bingley Local History Society have offered time, advice and access to their archives and photographs including those of Stanley Varo. Richard Freeman and Dale Smith of the Shipley Glen Tramway have pinpointed and provided research resources. Invaluable access to photographs and postcards has been provided by the Graham Hall Archives, Dorothy Burrows, Mick Walmsley of Woodbank Nurseries, Harden, Isabel, The Friends of Bingley College and Graham Carey. Original photographs have been provided by David Mitchell, John Steel Photography and Alex Homer.

Finally grateful thanks are offered to the readers of the local community magazine Prosider for their continued feedback and encouragement. Simon Harrup, Kimberley Devine and Chris Thorpe of Overt Marketing have been ever present sources of ideas and professional advice on the production and printing of this book and without them the project would never have reached fruition.

If anyone has not been acknowledged this is the fault of the author as are any inadvertent errors in the text. If any copyright has been infringed, apologies are offered as there has been no deliberate intent and every effort has been made to obtain permission, acknowledge and attribute content wherever possible.

**Alan Cattell**
**Bingley - December 2011**

# Introduction

For the casual visitor to Bingley and the surrounding area there are a number of artefacts and buildings which may provide more than just passing interest to the history of the local area. Bingley 5 Rise and 3 Rise Locks, Saltaire and Haworth Parsonage are amongst the most visited and important, but what else does the area offer in terms of history?

There are many examples of the quirky, the tragic or the local application of events which mirror historically what was happening at national level. Each of these had some effect on the local area and many of these have been forgotten in the mists of time. The intention of this book is to capture some of these forgotten "moments" and events and give context to how they impacted on or shaped Bingley and its "surrounds"

The book is divided into four Sections the content of which is summarised below:

## Section One - Time Line 1120 - 2011

To give context the book commences with a Time Line which covers events in Baildon, Bingley, Cottingley, Crossflats, Cullingworth, Eldwick, Harden, Haworth, Micklethwaite Morton, Saltaire, Shipley and Wilsden. This is intended to be illustrative rather than exhaustive. As a "road map" to the history of the local area from 1120 to 2011 it is intended to be a useful means of identifying and discovering links and patterns in history between each of these areas.

### Identification of Key Individuals

Neither Bingley nor its "surrounds" should be considered as isolated local communities divorced from the realities of what was happening nationally. National figures such as General Booth (Salvation Army) Charles Darwin, Charles Dickens, Benjamin Disraeli, David Livingston, William Morris, Mrs Pankhurst (Suffragetttes), Gabriel Dante- Rossetti and John Wesley to name but a few.... all had reason to visit Bradford and its local or nearby districts. At local level figures with a national profile such as the Bronte's and Titus Salt lived and worked in the area. The Timeline also identifies these individuals and the text covers the contributions of Disraeli, Morris and Rossetti locally.

## Section Two – The 1600's and 1700's

### Market and Transport

During this period the local economy was still reliant on agriculture as a main source of income for the landed gentry, their tenants and to support the local population. In Bingley there was an attempt to revive the fortunes of the local market endowed by Royal Charter in 1212 and Amended in 1697.

Increasing commercialisation during this period needed more efficient transport to speed up the supply of services and goods. This Section of the book will cover Bingley Market and the transport infrastructures introduced in the local area including Ireland Bridge, Road Building, Turnpikes and Stagecoaches and the building of the Leeds to Liverpool Canal through Bingley

## Section Two – The 1800's

### Industrialisation

This period saw increasingly competitive, local, national and worldwide markets and a need for greater speed and efficiency of manufacturing production. Development of new materials and technology saw the demise of old hand and craft skills.

The speed of industrial progress and the migration of workers from the land to "manufactories" led to an underclass of paupers and revision of the Poor Law and Corn Laws. Concern was shown in many quarters over the number of hours worked particularly by children in factories. During this period Bingley developed from a village into a town with an expanding population and a growing number of purpose built mills.

### Chartists

In the period 1838 to 1848 Bradford and District also became a centre for Chartist agitation where opportunities were spotted by the Chartists to recruit disenchanted workers to their cause. Chartist activity in 1842 (The Plug Plots) and 1848 (The Little Siege of Bingley) and their background are covered in this Section. Additionally, so is Bejamin Disraeli's visit to Bingley in 1844 in support of W B Ferrand the local landowner, Magistrate and a member of the national Parliamentary Tory "Young England" Party.

## Improvement

1847 proved to be an important year for Bingley as regards the building of the Midland Railway through the town. This and the constitution of the first Bingley Improvement Commission in the same year (to develop an infrastructure for the running of services to the town), where to prove key to its future.

1850 saw the forming of the Bingley Cooperative Society which over the next thirty years would open five Branches in local villages and seven Branches and a Central Store in Bingley. The opening of the Mechanics Institutes in Bingley and other villages to facilitate the learning and education of workers gives further evidence of community focussed effort.

## New Money – New Houses

The days of a local "squirearchy" in the Aire Valley were superseded by a number of local mill owners and industrialists donating new money, effort or leadership to either their workforce or to the local community. Amongst these (some of whom were regarded as Paternalists) were William Dunlop and John Aldam Heaton of Harden, Thomas Garnett and Alfred Sharp of Bingley and Titus Salt and Titus Salt Junior of Saltaire. Each was also in their own right a "patron of the arts" as regards furnishing the houses they either built or rented in the area. These houses and their decoration will also be described in this Section.

## Tragedy

Whilst there was much positive as regards change and improvement, 1869 saw a major disaster in Bingley in which 15 people including 8 schoolchildren, lost their lives. As a result a recommendation to Parliament was made by the Inquest Jury for a change in legislation as regards the safety of steam boilers, their operation and repair. The accident and its outcomes are described in this Section.

## Entertainment

Increasingly, local Victorians sought to escape the factory environment and pollution of towns and cities using the expanding railway system to explore the countryside. What is now known as Shipley Glen became a favourite location for a day out. The early days of the Glen and the development of the early rides and the much visited and loved Japanese Gardens are described as the conclusion to this Section.

## Section Four – The 1900's

In this Section individual events from each of the first four decades of the 1900's are described. The events of 1906 and 1920 cover the tragic death of a lady parachutist performing at a fund raising gala in Haworth, and the success then demise in the 1920's of what was called the Happy Valley Pleasure Resort at Harden.

1936 saw the German airship Hindenberg flying over the Aire Valley including Bingley on what was purported to be a spying mission. Or was it a humanitarian mission by a grieving relative in memory of his brother who as a prisoner of war had died at Morton during the 1919 flu epidemic?

The final event described is the first ever BBC broadcast in 1946 from what is now Beckfoot School, Bingley of a radio show called Have a Go. At its peak, the programme which was run at a different venue weekly attracted over twenty million listeners a week. The show was hosted by Halifax born Wilfred Pickles and was the idea of John Salt a BBC Executive who was the great grandson of Sir Titus Salt.

Such is the nature of history..... a famous family name from the 1800's linking with a radio "moment" of the 1940's!

# SECTION ONE

# A Timeline and Guide
to the History of Bingley and surrounding towns and villages

This Timeline is intended to capture some of the main events which have taken place in the local area from 1120 up to 2011. As such it is intended to be illustrative rather than exhaustive. Content from Chapters of this book is highlighted to give a sense of perspective and timescale.

| | |
|---|---|
| 1120 | Drax Priory grant Bingley Church |
| **1212** | **Bingley Market Charter granted - Page 25** |
| 1316 | Raids on Skipton by the Scots |
| 1500 | Bingley Church re-erected |
| 1503 | First Cottingley Hall built |
| 1518 | Bingley Church Choir erected |
| 1529 | Bingley Grammar School endowed |
| 1596 | Gawthorpe Hall, Bingley built |
| 1601 | Manor House, Micklethwaite built |
| 1616 | Harden Hall (St Ives) built |
| 1631 | Many inhabitants of Beckfoot hamlet die of the Black Plague |
| 1635 | Priestthorpe Hall (later known as the Old Vicarage) built |
| 1642 | Lord Thomas Fairfax (born in Otley) and his son rumoured to have stayed at Harden Hall during the Civil War |
| | East Riddlesden Hall built |

*Parish Church, Bingley*

*Market Hall, Main Street*

| 1677 | Eldwick Hall built |
|---|---|
| **1685** | **Ireland Bridge Bingley built of stone - Page 31** |
| 1723 | Beckfoot Bridge Bingley built |
| 1739 | Bingley Church Tower raised |
| **1753** | **Bingley Market Hall built on Main Street - Page 26** |
| | **Cottingley Toll Bar at Cottingley Bridge - Page 37** |
| 1757 | John Wesley visits and Bingley 13 times up to 1788 |
| 1770 | Myrtle Grove, Bingley built |
| | Regular gypsy gatherings are held at Baildon from this date and over the next 200 years |
| **1774** | **Leeds and Liverpool Canal – Skipton to Bingley opened including 3 and 5 Rise locks - Page 33** |
| **1775** | Roman silver coin horde found in a chest at Morton Banks by a local farmer |
| | **Ireland Bridge repaired and widened - Page 32** |
| 1780 | Haworth Parsonage Built |
| **1792** | Hewenden Mill- Wilsden built |
| | **First Stagecoaches through Bingley on Leeds to Kendal route, calling at the Kings Head, Elm Tree and White Horse coaching inns - Page 39** |
| 1794 | William Wickham of Cottingley acts as a British Master Spy during the French Revolution |
| 1796 | The Haworth highwayman James Sutcliffe is executed at York for highway robbery at Keighley |
| 1800 | Eldwick Beck Mill |

*Five Rise Locks*

*Haworth Parsonage*

1802    Providence Mill, Bingley

1810    Holroyd Mill, Morton Beck

1812    Prospect Mill, Bingley

1814    Building of Bingley Elementary School

1815    Old Chapel , High Eldwick

1820    Bronte family move to Haworth

**1823**    Shipley St John's Church foundation stone laid

    **Toll Bar moved to Cottingley Bar - Page 37**

1824    St Matthews Church, Wilsden foundation stone laid

**1825**    **Opening of the Keighley to Bradford Turnpike Road - Page 37**

1828    Sunday School, Wilsden

1830    The Airedale Heifer weighing 41 stone 12 pounds and owned by Mr Slingsby of Riddlesden Hall is slaughtered

1832    Spring Mill, Wilsden

1836    Titus Salt discovers practical use for Alpaca wool

1837    Mechanics Institute, Wilsden

1839    Infants School, Wilsden

1841    Providence Mill, Wilsden

**1842**    **Plug Drawing on water and steam at Bingley mills by the Chartists - Page 49**

**1843**    Royd Mill, Wilsden

    **Friday 13th April John Nicholson – the Airedale Poet and an employee of Titus Salt dies of exposure after falling into the River Aire near Victoria Road, Saltaire - Page 123**

**1844**    **Benjamin Disraeli -future Prime Minister opens Bingley and Cottingley Allotments - Page 51**

1845    Charlotte Bronte applies for a job as Governess to the Thornton family at Cottingley Old Hall but is turned down because she is not musically talented

1846    Shipley Railway Station

**1847**    **Shipley to Keighley line opened including Bingley and Keighley stations - Page 58**

*Bingley Station*

*Dick Hudsons*

**First Bingley Improvement Commisioners - Page 40**

1848    Bankfield, Bingley (now a hotel) built

**Chelsea Pensioners defend Bingley during Chartist march and arrests of the ringleaders - Page 64**

1850    Opening of Fleece Inn, Eldwick – run by Dick Hudson as Landlord until 1878. Now known as Dick Hudsons

Bingley Co-operative Society formed

1851    Bingley Building Society founded

Great Wilsden flood

1852    Cottingley Mechanics Institute

New Primitive Methodist Chapel, Ryecroft

**1853**    Salts Mill opened on 20th September, Titus Salts 50th birthday

**Charles Dickens publishes an article in Household Words calling Titus Salt "The Great Yorkshire Llama" as a playful reference to his use of alpaca wool - Page 35**

1854    Saltaire Village – first building phase completed

Charles Dickens visits Saltaire during the building

1856    Saltaire railway station opened

1857    Saltaire Village – second building phase completed

Richard Thornton of Cottingley invited by Livingstone to accompany him on his Zambesi expedition

1858    William Napier of Bingley awarded the Victoria Cross for valour during the Indian Mutiny

1859    Charles Darwin stayed at Ilkley from October to December. His book Origin of the Species was published in November

Mechanics Institute Harden

*Mechanics Institute*

*Bingley Boiler Explosion*

Cullingworth and Crossflatts Co-ops opened

Bowling Green Mill, Bingley

Boathouse Saltaire opened

1875  Micklethwaite Free Methodist Chapel

1876  Baildon Station built and Shipley to Guiseley railway opened

Wilsden and Crossflats schools opened

1877  Board Schools opened at Mornington Road, Bingley, Eldwick and Harden

Bingley Rugby founded

1878  Harden Co-op opened

1880  Airedale Harriers founded

**1882**  Royal visit to Saltaire by the Prince and Princess of Wales

**Bingley Market Rights purchased from Lord of Manor - Page 28**

Cullingworth Viaduct opened

1884  Hewenden Viaduct built and Cullingworth and Denholme railway stations built

1886  Wilsden station opened

**1887**  Exhibition Building Saltaire opened and **Jubilee Exhibition** opened by Prince Henry Of Batenberg and HRH Princess Beatrice - **Page 92, 98, 101 & 109**

Central Co-op store built on Bingley Main Street

**1888**  **Market Hall and butter cross moved from Main Street, Bingley to the quarry in Prince of Wales Park - Page 28**

Elm Tree Hill removed for widening of Main Street, Bingley

1889  Bingley Technical School opened

Post Office building Wilsden built but never used as a Post Office

1890  Methodist Church, Wilsden built and Bingley Cottage Hospital opened

1891  Midland Hotel, Bingley built

Baildon Golf Club founded

**1892**  **Bingley Free Library opened - Page 75**

*General Booth in Bingley 1907*

| 1911 | Prince's Hall Cinema, Shipley |
| | Bingley Ladies Teacher Training College opened |
| **1913** | **Bingley Post Office, Main Street - Page 29** |
| | Cottingley Toll House demolished and Cottingley Bridge widened |
| | Hippodrome Cinema, Bingley |
| 1914 | First Tram into Bingley |
| 1915 | Shipley Cinema |
| 1917 | Baildon Picture House |
| | Photographs of Cottingley Fairies taken by two local girls endorsed as real by Sir Arthur Conan Doyle. Later disproved |
| 1918 | Tom Duxbury opens a firelighter shop on Whitley Street, Bingley which expands into joinery manufacturing and eventually becomes Magnet Joinery |
| | Ryshworth and Crossflatts housing sites acquired |
| 1919 | Betty's Cafe, Ilkley |
| | Harden housing site |
| **1920** | Northcliffe Woods, Shipley opened |
| | Cullingworth and Wilsden housing sites |
| | Saltaire Park given to Council by Sir James Roberts |
| | **Happy Valley Pleasure Grounds open at Harden - Page 126** |
| 1921 | Bandstand, Northcliffe Woods, Shipley |
| | Myrtle Cinema, Bingley (now the Myrtle Grove Pub) |
| 1922 | Saltaire Cinema |
| **1927** | Opening of Princess Hall and Swimming Baths at Bingley by the Earl of Harewood and HRH Princess Mary |
| | Cottingley Housing site |

*Bingley Teacher Training College*

*Hindenberg over Harden*

*Cullingworth Station*

| 1957 | Saltaire Cinema closed |
|------|------------------------|
| 1960 | Baildon Picture House closed |
| | Arndale Shopping Centre, Shipley opened |
| 1962 | Bingley Building Society Head Office |
| | New Market Hall, Shipley opened |
| 1963 | Salts Grammar School |
| 1964 | Bradford and Bingley formed from the merger of the Bradford Equitable and Bingley |
| | Permanent Building Societies |
| 1965 | Damart Factory at Bingley |
| | Saltaire station closes |
| **1970** | Airedale General Hospital |
| | Major redevelopment of Central Area of Bingley comprising Myrtle Grove, Chapel Lane, Main Street and 7 Dials areas of Bingley (continued through to 1974). **Building of Myrtle Walk Shopping Centre - Page 30** |
| 1972 | Shipley Baths |
| **1973** | **Bingley Library and small Market opens in new Myrtle Walk Shopping Precinct - Page 30** |
| | Baildon Station reopened |
| 1974 | Bingley UDC dissolved – Becomes Bingley Ward of Bradford Council |
| | Demolition of Holy Trinity Church, Bingley |
| | Bingley Little Theatre moves to new Bingley Arts Centre |
| 1976 | Victoria Hall, Bingley demolished |
| | Wilsden Village Hall |
| **1977** | **Jubilee Gardens, Bingley - Page 30** |
| | Princess Ann visits Saltaire |
| 1979 | Bingley College closed |
| | Salts Hospital closed |
| 1982 | Crossflats Station |
| | Yorkshire Clinic |

*Bingley Relief Road, Railway and Canal, 2010*

# SECTION
# TWO

1600's and 1700's

# Eight Hundred Years of Bingley Market

**In 2012 Bingley will celebrate the eight hundredth anniversary of being awarded its first Market Charter. This chapter traces the key events and dates for the Bingley Market Hall and Butter Cross since 1212.**

The granting of the Charter elevated the status of Bingley to that of a Market Town with important implications for its subsequent growth and development.

### What was a Butter Cross?

A Butter Cross was a type of market cross dating from medieval times. Its name originated from the fact that the cross would be located at a local market place, sometimes near a church or a manor where people would come to buy and sell locally produced butter, milk and eggs. In Bingley's case the original market is likely to have been held in the churchyard as was customary elsewhere (Dodd 1958 *Bingley*). The fresh produce would be laid out and displayed on the circular stepped base of the cross.

Design of crosses varied from place to place, but they were often covered by some type of roof to offer shelter, although these were mostly added at a much later date than the original cross that they covered. *The 1966 Grade II* listing of the Bingley Butter Cross states that although its date is uncertain, it was possibly 13th Century in origin. The roof was however added in 1753.

### The First Market Charter

On 19th May 1212 King John declared "*by the Grace of God know ye that we have granted and by this our Charter confirmed to Maurice de Gant that he have one market at his Manor of Bingley every week on Sunday. So nevertheless that the same market be not to the injury of the neighbouring markets. Wherefore we will and firmly command that the aforesaid Maurice and his heirs have the aforesaid market in the aforesaid manor of Bingley for ever well and in peace, freely and quietly with all liberties and free customs belonging to such market pertaining as is aforesaid.*"

The statement above was intended to do a number of things:

• Establish the day on which the market would be held

• Ensure that a new market town could not be established too close to an existing one. A limit, usually a day's worth of travelling to and from the market, for buying or selling goods, was established as a rule of thumb. This was done to try and ensure fair practice.

• Ensure that the person to whom the Charter was granted and their heirs in perpetuity ran the market in an orderly, fair and equitable manner.

## The Second Market Charter (Or Ammendment)

The fact that there is little or no documentation during the medieval period specifically relating to the market would point towards the fact that it possibly satisfied the needs of the local community and the above requirements.

A Second Market Charter was granted by William and Mary in 1693. This related to holding a market on Monday each week and is likely to have been an amendment to the first charter as these were more common than entirely new endowments. As a result the main elements of the original Market Hall were constructed following the Second Market Charter. The exact date of its construction is not known but it is reasoned that this must have been sometime between 1693 and 1753 when it is recorded that two new bays to the Market Hall were built (*1966 Grade II Listing and Bingley Conservation Area Assessment 2004*).

*Market Hall on Main Street*

Dodd (1958) confirms that *"The Market Hall was standing on Main Street (a little lower than the place from which it was removed in 1888) at least as early as 1720, when it was reported that the market day was Monday"* He also notes that *"The market rights still fell to the Lord of the Manor and the Hall became his property, though the cost of building or possibly rebuilding, fell on the town."*

## 1753

What is without doubt is that Thomas Lister a local builder carried out renovation and additions *"at considerable expense"* namely twelve pounds thirteen shillings and ten and a half pence in 1753. Local accounts confirm that the cross was already there and that the work entailed roofing the cross and adding the two bays to the market hall and an archway with a dated keystone. Mention is also made that the market was *"furnished"* with standard weights and measures, the scales and weights being owned by the Manor Court. An early example of controlled Weights and Measures!

## 1775

By1775 an effort was made to try to revive the flagging fortunes of the market *"which had for some time been lost"* despite the money that had been spent on it. The intention was to make Bingley a rural market town of note.

A committee of 14 which included leading landowners was formed to look at reorganising the way that the market was run. As a result new resolutions were made to try and improve usage:

• The market would be held every Tuesday and the 100 signatories of the resolutions pledged that for a year they would not buy grain, dairy goods, vegetables anywhere other than the Public Market.

• Customers should "refrain" from buying meat off any butcher who "shall refuse to erect a stall in the neighbourhood of the Market Cross" This was also intended to dissuade customers from buying directly from farmers.

• Every effort would be made to persuade travelling dealers in hardware, hats and fish from neighbouring towns and villages to sell their goods at the market.

## Changing Times

Unfortunately despite these efforts, market activity was not revived and the situation actually got worse. An outbreak of the Black Plague in 1787 resulted in many local farmers transferring their business to the market at Otley.

In 1806 the market appears to have no longer been in existence but it opened again before 1822 with Tuesday as the market day. Horsfall Turner (1897) reports that in 1830 the Market was still being held on Tuesday in its position near the Old Queens Head on Main Street. Dodd (1958) however reports that by 1837 Bingley was an industrial rather than market centre *"greatly declined from its former consequence."*

## The Stocks

Up to 1818 the Bingley Stocks had been situated near the Parish Church but in that year they had new stone posts fitted at a cost of five shillings and were moved to Main Street next to the Butter Cross and the Market Hall. The stocks were last used in 1870 but to this day remain with the Butter Cross and Market Hall.

*Market Hall, Butter Cross and Stocks*

## Purchase of the Market Rights

On May 28th 1868 The Leeds Mercury announced that the Market would be transferred to Myrtle Place and would take place on Saturday evenings. From this date onwards the ancient market relics of Bingley situated in Main Street would become subject to much change.

This was pre-empted in August 1882 when the Ancient Market Rights were purchased from George Lane-Fox, the then Lord of the Manor by the Bingley Improvement Commissioners for £800. Amongst improvements suggested were the widening of Main Street necessitating the removal of the old market buildings because *"For many years the old Market House, Butter Cross and Wesleyan Chapel quite blocked one portion of the chief thoroughfare rendering the passage of vehicles difficult and not altogether free of danger."*

*"The Market House was in 1888 removed stone by stone and re-erected at the top of Prince of Wales Park where it now remains. The old Butter Cross and Stocks were removed thither at the same time"* (Dodd 1958). John Brown

*Market Hall, Butter Cross and Stocks in Prince of Wales Park*

was paid sixteen pounds and six shillings for reconstructing them on site. The buildings would no longer be used as a market and would remain in the Park for a further 96 years.

In respect of a location for the new market Dodd (1958) records *"the suggestion of Myrtle Place* (though in 1868 its use as a market place on Saturdays had been permitted) *was rejected as it was the only outlet where boys could play and people hold meetings. Mr Ferrand offered a site opposite the Parish Church but this was also rejected."*

## Market Bye Laws

To ensure that the administration and running of the market would protect the interests of the community and of traders, in September 1895 a new set of Bye-Laws in the Urban District of Bingley were written and introduced. It would appear that a "temporary" market building known as "the shed" provided a home for the market until it was demolished to make way for the new Post Office on Main Street in 1913.

From then on Myrtle Place was the natural home in the centre of Bingley for the market which became firmly established and ran on Fridays each week.

*"The Shed"*

## Further Change

Subsequently when Myrtle Place was demolished for improvements in the 1970's the Market moved to the Myrtle Walk Shopping Centre in 1973. Here it existed as a small covered area outside the Library entrance until the redesign of the Centre as Bingley 5 Rise Precinct in December 2009.

The Civic Trust moved the Market Hall, Butter Cross and Stocks back into the centre of Bingley to Jubilee Gardens at a cost of £18,000 in 1984. On 22nd September 1984 the buildings were handed back to Bradford Council.

The last move of Bingley Market was to the Town Square near Bingley Little Theatre in March 2008 where it now runs as an Open Market on Wednesday, Friday and Saturday each week.

## 2011

So, in 2011 a market still exists in the centre of Bingley with the ancient market relics beside it as a historic reminder. Despite the passage of time, the market still suffers the vagaries of fluctuations in trade and increasing competition from supermarkets and local traders, each trying to survive in the face of an economic downturn.

However, 800 years of local service is a legacy that few institutions are likely to be able to match!

# Ireland Bridge

Bingley.                                    Ireland Bridge.

Fords or bridges across rivers have played an important part in the siting of towns and villages throughout history. In the case of the Bingley area Cottingley Bridge, Beckfoot Bridge and Ireland Bridge have long been crossing points.

## Wooden Bridge

The area below Ireland Bridge was originally an ancient ford. Up to 1685 there was a narrow wooden bridge structure for horses and for foot passengers. At this stage there were few wheeled vehicles such as carts and the bridge was primarily used by drovers and pack horses who regularly crossed the Aire at this point. Records of the time describe it as *"A wood-bridge, and only passable by horse or foote, not by carte, and goes up a hill to the moores, an obscure way not used by any strangers as we are informed."*

What we might now describe as social networking also took place at the site. Speight (1898) in *Chronicles and Stories of Old Bingley* observes *"Formerly it was the rendezvous of the gossips of the town, for here young and old were wont to congregate and gather news from passing travellers and from the drovers of pack horses who regularly crossed this way between Otley, Ilkley and the villages between Bingley and Halifax."*

Speight also suggests that the bridge was known as Ireland Bridge because the river Aire at this point separated two manors and ownerships of land "*and to cross the water was a facetious comparison with the passage over the channel between England and Ireland.*"

In 1685 a discussion took place between the Parish of Bingley and the West Riding as to who was responsible for the cost of rebuilding and repair of the bridge and the following pronouncement was made:

*Indictment at Wakefield, Jan. 1685. Indictment Book.*

*Records of this Court, &c. The Jury found it an ancient Riding Bridge. To be viewed & cost of rebuilding ascertained and certified & 200 estr. 270 estreated. Charged as a Riding Bridge.*

## Stone Bridge

Accordingly the wooden bridge was replaced with a dressed stone one in 1685 at a cost of £270. Records show that because of increased usage by wheeled vehicles (the volume of which had not been anticipated) the bridge had to be repaired and widened in 1775 as it was "*very ruinous, narrow and in great decay.*"

In essence this is the last recorded major and substantial repair of the original stone bridge. Interesting when we consider that this was 236 years ago, which could not possibly take account of the invention of the motor car, nor the utilisation of the bridge as a major crossing point not an "obscure way" as historically described.

In 2011 the bridge, a Grade II listed structure due to its age, rarity and quality was restored, widened and strengthened. The importance of the siting of the bridge and the convenience of using it was brought home to many commuters who had to make considerably longer journeys for the period that it was closed.

Ireland Bridge 2011

Perhaps this chapter might put a historical context and perspective on the inconvenience people complained of at the time! As with most notable events in Bingley's history, past and present provide us with direct parallels.

# Bingley and the Canal Network

In the mid 1700's Bingley was at the hub of a number of communications networks including several pack horse routes, a Turnpike system and the Leeds, Bradford and Kendal coaching routes. In terms of cost, time and capability to transport larger quantities of goods an alternative to traditional "road" routes was needed. As such canals were developed to provide an efficient and cheap way of transporting bulk goods, such things as coal, limestone and soap.

Additionally a means of linking the waterways from the East Coast and Hull across Yorkshire and Lancashire to Liverpool was considered as necessary. This would allow passage between Europe and the Irish and North seas' as well as enabling access to export/import routes to growing markets in Africa and America via Liverpool. In the event, the canal in its entirety took forty six years to complete due to its length and complexity in satisfying the needs of a number of different stakeholders.

At local level the trade in lime and coal between Bradford and Skipton was an important element of the economy of the Aire Valley and as such formed part of the discussions around the need for a local canal system.

## The Skipton – Bingley Connection

An advertisement in the Leeds Mercury in 1741 invited the gentlemen of Airedale who lived between Skipton and Bingley to a meeting at the Golden Lion in Kildwick to consider *"whether or not it will be beneficial to this part of the country to make the River Aire navigable for carrying and recarrying of Coal and Lime and other small Branches of Trade from Gargrave in Craven down to Cottingley Bridge in the Parish of Bingley."*

Local politics on both sides of the Pennines were a feature of the negotiations throughout the building of the canal and the needs and interests of local landowners dictated that the Bingley to Skipton connection took until 1773 to achieve. On 8th April of that year the Leeds Intelligencer reported

*"On Thursday last, that part of the Grand Canal from Bingley to Skipton was opened, and two boats laden with coals arrived at the last mentioned place, which were sold at half the price they have hitherto given for that most necessary convenience of life, which is a recent instance, among other, of the great use of canals in general. On which occassion the bells were set ringing at*

33

*Skipton; there were also bonfires, illuminations, and other demonstrations of joy.*"

## The Bingley Locks

On 21st March 1774 the Skipton to Thackley connection which included the staircase locks at Bingley was opened and the first boat down the Five Rise Locks took 28 minutes. 30,000 people are reported to have attended the event and a local holiday was declared. The Leeds Intelligencer reported

*"From Bingley to about 3 miles downwards the noblest works of the kind are exhibited viz: A five fold, a three fold and a single lock, making together a fall of 120 feet; a large aqueduct bridge of seven arches over the River Aire and an aqueduct and banking over the Shipley valley ....... This joyful and much wished for event was welcomed with the ringing of Bingley bells, a band of music, the firing of guns by the neighbouring Militia, the shouts of spectators, and all the marks of satisfaction that so important an acquisition merits."*

The lock system was designed by John Longbotham of Halifax and built by local stonemasons : Barnabus Morvill, Jonathan Farrar, William Wild all of Bingley and John Sugden from Wilsden. The locks raise boats 59ft 2in over a distance of 320ft. Firth (1999) in *The Leeds and Liverpool Canal in Yorkshire* notes that a plentiful supply of water was a prerequisite of the siting of the locks as each lock holds between 80,000 and 90,000 gallons when full.

*Bingley Five Rise*

At its summit the Leeds and Liverpool Canal surmounted a level of 411 feet four inches above the river Aire which it joined at Leeds. The stretch from Shipley to Bingley covered difficult terrain of which the Three and Five Rise Locks at Bingley provided stepped access to the flatter stretch of countryside running along the side of the valley up to Skipton.

## Then and Now

The building of Salts Mill at Saltaire took full advantage of the canal (and later the railway system) to enable Titus Salt to import the Alpacca wool for which he was famous from South America, through Liverpool and by canal to the Aire Valley. Charles Dickens who visited Saltaire penned an article on Titus calling him "The Great Yorkshire Llama" because of his affinity for the wool. In respect of providing a link to Hull, Liverpool and beyond, Saltaire is a prime example of the successful location of the canal and its effect on developing industrialisation.

Over 200 years later, the canal and locks are still in daily use in providing access for a range of pleasure craft accessing the Yorkshire Dales and Skipton. Additionally the canal tow path serves as a walking and cycling route to tourists and the local community and in September 2009 was designated the Airedale Greenway route. Connections are also possible through the railway stations located right the way up the Aire Valley.

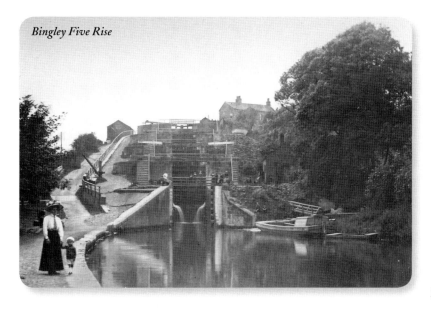

*Bingley Five Rise*

# Transport through Bingley – Turnpike Roads and Stagecoaches

**This Chapter traces the development of road networks and faster means of travel and transport of goods and passengers in the local area.**

## Transport Links

Transport links between major towns and locations originally developed by the Romans were preceded by highways to meet local community needs and by ancient ridge ways and pack horse routes. Local highways generally followed valley bottoms and were often subject to  flooding and the vagaries of the weather. For centuries most of the roads in the Pennines and Dales were in an appalling condition, particularly in the winter when they became too muddy and rutted. From 1555, parishes like Bingley were made responsible for the maintenance of their own roads.

## Pack Horse Routes

In contrast pack horse trails usually traversed across valleys, taking the shortest but not always easiest routes across exposed moorland tops. In the Dales and Pennines these routes usually ran east to west and were used for carrying wool, lead, lime and coal to markets outside the area and bringing necessities such as salt back in.

Local examples are the Bingley to Ilkley packhorse trail, the main packhorse route between Keighley and Halifax and the route between Haworth and Colne. In 1667 local justices were ordered to erect guide posts on the moors where routes intersected and many of these still exist today on rambling routes. The narrow flag paved paths were known as 'causeys". These routes are still a feature of the Pennine landscape.

Pack horse trails were generally wide enough to allow horses or mules to move in single file. Where the track crossed a river a pack horse bridge would be constructed to allow for animals carrying panniers containing transported goods. These bridges were hump backed for added strength.

In the Bingley area Beckfoot Packhorse Bridge and Ford were sited on the oldest road in the district which was originally an ancient forest road along the river bank from Cottingley. This represented the old packhorse route from the lower Aire Valley to Bingley. As trade grew, pack horses became increasingly inadequate because this was a slow and relatively

costly mode of transport
with the serious limitation
that so little could be
carried on the back of
a horse. Consequently
alternative and more
competitive means of
transport were sought.

*Early Pack Horse Bridge*

## Turnpike Roads

The increasing need
to transport greater quantities
of heavy goods over long distances more quickly meant that
eventually packhorse routes were simply not adequate enough. Methods
of improving the poor state of repair of existing roads also needed to be
looked at.

In 1727 the first Turnpike Trusts were set up by Acts of Parliament to
speed up travel and to improve the state of repair of roads. Money for
road improvement was raised by charging users tolls at the Toll Gate or
Toll Bar. This is essentially the same system as is used nowadays in the
USA and on some of the newly built toll motorways in the UK.

In 1752 the Act for Making and Improving the Keighley and Kendal
Turnpike Road was granted. In 1753 a Toll Bar was erected at Cottingley
Bridge to include the Keighley to Bradford route up Bradford Old Road
and over the moor. This Toll Bar was later moved to the junction of the
new branch road from Shipley to Bingley in 1823.

The introduction of toll gates was resented by local communities who
had freely used the routes for centuries. New tolls on old roads sparked
protests known as the Rebecca Riots. All over the country mobs
destroyed bar gates and the one at Cottingley also came under attack.
These different groups of attackers were often led by a "Rebecca" dressed
in women's clothing and the followers often dressed similarly to disguise
themselves.

Local accounts reported "*Mobs gathered from Otley, Yeadon and most of the
valleys of Airedale and proceeded to pull down the gates at Apperley Bridge,
Kirkstall, Bingley and Leeds.*" Toll charges also prohibited many of the
poor from using the turnpikes leading one Bradford observer to state
"*The turnpikes were, by the lower class, universally regarded as an obnoxious*

37

*Bar House Cottingley*

*regulation – more adopted for the wealthy portion of the community whose carriages could hardly pass on the old roads."*

Examples of fees charged for the use of Turnpikes in the Bradford area are:

| | |
|---|---|
| *Six horses or more* | *24 pence* |
| *Five horses* | *15 pence* |
| *Reducing to:* | |
| *One horse* | *3 pence* |
| *For every additional animal* | *2 pence* |
| *Oxen* | *10 pence a score* |
| *Calves and hogs* | *5 pence a score* |

These rates were daily charges, with exemptions given for people voting in parliamentary elections, vehicles carrying repair materials for the turnpikes, vehicles carrying farm produce and implements, and for churchgoers. Whilst the turnpikes undoubtedly helped commerce in the area, they were less useful in the development of heavy goods transport.

From 1767, mileposts were compulsory on all turnpikes, to inform travellers of direction and distances, to help coaches keep to schedule and for charging for changes of horses at the coaching inns. The distances were also used to calculate postal charges before the uniform postal rate was introduced in 1840.

## Stagecoaches

Stage coaches were vehicles generally drawn by four horses which could seat four or six people inside, and twelve on the roof. A stage was a point where the horses were changed; generally stages were at between ten and fifteen mile intervals. Stage-coaches were of several kinds- stage coach proper, mail coach, road coach and private coach. The heyday of the vehicle was from 1784 when the Post Office began sending mail by this means. By the end of the 18th century, travel by stage coach was becoming more common in England, especially for the middle and upper classes.

## Bingley Coaching Inns

Bingley was situated on a number of major coaching routes, with coaches departing to Leeds, Bradford  Skipton, Settle, Kendal and Lancaster and to Colne, Blackburn, Crosshills and Preston from the town's three coaching inns. On the Leeds to Kendal route Bingley was a half way point between Leeds and Skipton, being 15 miles from each and therefore represented a perfect place to stop and change horses.

Downsborough (2009) in *The Lost Pubs of Bingley*, records that in 1792 one of the earliest stage coaches, the Packet used the Kings Head pub at Bingley to change horses. Other Bingley pubs used as coaching inns were the White Horse and the Elm Tree. In 2011 only the White Horse remains.

## Demise of the Turnpike System

By 1830 there were more than 1000 turnpike roads in England alone, many connected with the stagecoach network. Unfortunately many roads were dangerous because highwaymen often used them to rob stagecoaches. In the local area Nab Wood was identified as a particularly vulnerable area. Records at York Assizes show that John Sutcliffe of Haworth was arrested for highway robbery and executed at York for stealing a parcel containing sixty pounds, several notes and bills.

The new and developing railway systems could by the late 1840's provide safer, faster and more comfortable travel, at the expense of the turnpike roads and stagecoaches. Tolls on the Keighley and Bradford Turnpike Road were eventually discontinued in 1868.

## Links with the Canal System

The classic period of stagecoaches lasted from about 1810 to the early 1850s. However not all stagecoaches existed as separate entities. With an eye to business at least one of the stagecoach companies ensured a link between stagecoaches and the canal system (which originally came to Bingley in 1774).

Horsfall-Turner (1897) writing in *Ancient Bingley* comments: *"Coach travelling though very expensive became frequent for those who could afford it. Amongst the most noted coaches passing through Bingley, we hear of the Packet 1792 -1800 on Monday, Wednesday and Friday at 9am, to Bradford and Bingley where the passengers and luggage were transferred to the canal boat to proceed to Skipton. The fare for inside the coach and front cabin from Leeds to Skipton was six shillings and sixpence; outside the coach and back cabin three shillings and sixpence. Mr Maude of the Old Kings Arms managed the Bingley end."*

## The Railway System

Travel in the local area was to change radically with the building of railway links throughout the Aire and Worth Valleys. The effects on Bingley and the introduction of a railway station in 1847 are covered on page 58. Road systems through Bingley would later be reviewed by the Bingley Improvement Commissioners who were first constituted in 1847.

## Later changes to the Roads in Bingley

Prior to 1865 what is now Park Road was called Toad Lane on account of it being a thoroughfare for toads migrating between the two Bingley Bog swamp areas. In 1865 the building of the new Prince of Wales Park led to the road being renamed Park Road.

By the 1880's the main road through Bingley was in need of significant change identified by the Bingley Improvement Commissioners. On one hand the stretch from what is now from the corner of Park Road down to just past the Fleece Inn was narrowed by a Wesleyan Chapel, shops and the Butter Cross, Market and Stocks, and was considered dangerous. This was addressed by removal of the latter to Prince of Wales Park in 1888. Additionally one of Bingley's older streets Elm Tree Hill was also removed and pavements were dug up and the road widened.

The second change took place in 1904 when buildings at the top of what was then in essence the original Main Street through Bingley (opposite the White Horse Inn) and along towards the Parish Church were demolished. To do so needed an Act of Parliament in 1903. The road to Keighley was then widened and placed on the right hand side of the Church which required the removal 2483 bodies from the graveyard. A small portion of the original graveyard can still be seen to the right of the Keighley Road opposite the Church.

*Pavement removal and road widening, Main Street 1886*

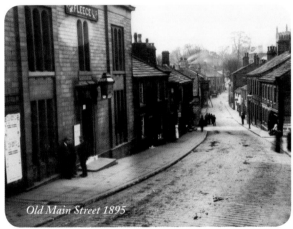

*Old Main Street 1895*

*New road 1904*

# SECTION
# THREE

## The 1800's

# Chartism in Bradford and Bingley – The Plug Plots

Chartism was a national movement that was particularly well supported in the North of England and in the textile and industrial towns of Lancashire and Yorkshire. Wright (1987) *The Chartist Risings in Bradford* points out that although Chartism was a national movement, its strength lay in the fact that it was successful because of support from activists at local level.

He also identifies that in each of the three peaks of Chartist activity, namely 1839-1840, 1842 and 1848, Home Office papers identified that the Government regarded Bradford as a potential hotbed of revolution.

**This chapter is intended to give a National context to Chartism whilst also examining local support for Chartism in the Bradford and Bingley areas.**

### Why did Chartism seem to be a threat to authority?

To the Government the Chartists represented a potential force capable of the upheaval and overthrow of social institutions and authority similar to the French Revolution. With that in mind, rather than being persuaded by the sensibilities of the Chartist's demands, they reacted in fear at the possibility of violent overthrow of society - and their own positions of authority.

*Chartists riots*

## Why Chartism?

Nationally the stimulation for Chartism appeared to lie in the inequities of the Reform Bill 1832 where it was regarded by many that the middle classes but not the working classes had been admitted into the parliamentary system. The Bill was seen as a betrayal of a large section of the population, thus creating some of the resentment and anger that led to Chartism.

The Poor Law of 1834 was seen as an attack on the working class and their fear and hatred of the workhouse. There were other injustices, including the treatment of trade unionists, to fan the flames that turned people into Chartists.

However there were many other contributory and complex factors relevant to different parts of the country. Those specific to Bradford and District are shown in the Table on page 47.

## Approaches to Chartism

There were two main approaches to Chartism:

That of the "moral force" Chartists who advocated more peaceful methods of persuasion and protest such as the presentation of petitions to Parliament to convince those in power that there needed to be changes in the Parliamentary system.

The "physical force" Chartists who as the name implies intended to force change by more physical and possibly violent means. It was regarded that the Bradford Chartists were in the main within this category.

Briggs (1960) in *Chartist Studies* however counselled historians to recognise that the all-embracing concept of the six points of the 1838 Peoples Charter motivated different social groups in different times and places with differing degrees of intensity.

## The Charter

The People's Charter was published in May 1838 and proponents of the charter gathered over 1.25 million signatures in support of their aims. These and the Charter which detailed six key points (shown below) were presented to Parliament when it met in July 1939.

- Universal suffrage (the right to vote) for every man 21 years of age.
- Abolition of property qualifications for members of parliament to enable constituencies to return the man of their choice, rich or poor.

- Annual parliamentary elections as a check on bribery and intimidation.
- Equal representation, securing the same amount of representation for the same number of electors rather than allowing small constituencies to swamp the votes of large ones.
- Payment of members of parliament to help any tradesman, working or other person to serve a constituency when taken from his business to serve the needs of the country.
- Vote by secret ballot to protect the elector in the exercise of his vote.

The Commons rejected the Charter by 235 votes to 46. Future Prime Minister Benjamin Disraeli took the opportunity to affirm that whilst he disproved of the Charter he sympathised with the Chartists. Disraeli as a leading advocate of a Parliamentary group called Young England would visit Bingley in 1844 to support local squire and a fellow MP, William Busfeild Ferrand.

# NATIONAL CHARTER ASSOCIATION
## OF
## GREAT BRITAIN,

Established for the purpose of effecting, by peaceable and Constitutional means, the Representation of the whole Male Adult population of the United Kingdom in the Commons House of Parliament, by the enactment of the Bill, entitled

### THE PEOPLE'S CHARTER,

which contains the following fundamentals for the establishment of a just form of Government :

UNIVERSAL SUFFRAGE-VOTE BY BALLOT-ANNUAL PARLIAMENTS-
NO PROPERTY QUALIFICATION-PAYMENT OF MEMBERS-
AND EQUAL ELECTORAL DISTRICTS.

184____

Entered ____

Name ____

PHILIP McGRATH, President.
CHRISTOPHER DOYLE, Secretary.

### The Dissolution of the Chartists National Convention.

The first gathering of Chartist delegates had taken place in London in February 1839 and included a delegate from Bradford. Divisions that were to trouble Chartistism in general were already very apparent, as some delegates favoured violence if necessary, some favoured a general strike, and there was even talk of electing a "people's parliament. A motto adopted at the Convention *"peaceably if we may, forcibly if we must,"* may have frightened off those more moderate middle-class members who might have been persuaded to support their cause.

During 1839 the government took the opportunity to have many leaders of the movement arrested, or detained including William Lovett (Moral Force) and Fergus O'Connor (Physical Force). Both were jailed for seditious libel, Lovett for 12 months and O'Connor for 18 months (in York) There were also outbreaks of violence in several regions, notably at Newport, where 24 protestors were killed.

### Bradford Chartists

The rise of Chartism in Bradford was a combination of many factors including those above and in addition: de-skilling of traditional textile skills, introduction of new technology, economic depression, wage reductions, unemployment, domination of industry by large employers, Anti Poor Law feelings and support for the10 Hour Act to name but a few. The Table opposite details some the main factors in the order in which they occurred.

### 1842 The Presentation of the Second Petition

In May 1842 Thomas Duncombe who was an MP in the House of Commons and a friend of Lovett agreed to present a Chartist petition signed by over 3.2 million people, to Parliament. As a Moral Force Chartist he was prepared to argue the case for universal suffrage. As well as demanding the six points of the Charter the document also expressed concern about factory conditions, liberty and church taxes on "noncomformists."

Again the House of Commons decided not to accept the petition by 287 votes to 47.

### The General Strike

In 1842 there was a General Strike, due to a downturn in trade and a consequent economic depression. This in turn caused unemployment

# Events which influenced Chartism in Bradford and District

| Year | Event | Outcome |
|------|-------|---------|
| 1822 | Bradford manufacturer secretly constructs a power loom at Shipley - Destroyed | Fear of de-skilling by hand craftsmen, wage reductions and unemployment because of new machinery |
| 1825 | Bradford Strike of wool combers and handloom weavers for 23 weeks. Union formation | Loss of control over wages, wage level and conditions. Large employers begin to dominate the industry |
| 1829 | Founding of the Bradford Political Union (BPU) | Dissatisfaction with the new industrial system, coming of textile machinery, hostility towards an uninformed political system |
| 1830 | BPU furthered by involvement in 10 Hour Factory agitation | Richard Oastler involved |
| Early 1830s | Concern over hours worked in the new factories | Trade unionists and radical factory reformers increasingly involved |
| 1832 | Bradford open to a deepening politicisation of the population due to 1832 Reform Act | The parliamentary reform of 1832 gave little assistance to the Bradford workforce |
| April 1832 | Workers from Leeds, Bradford, Bingley, Keighley and other West Yorkshire towns walk to York | Demonstration in support of a 10 Hours Bill |
| 1835 | Feargus O'Connor visits West Riding. Vigour of 10 Hour movement and opposition to Poor Law in North of England | Northern working class hated new Poor Law. Bradford was the centre of the Anti Poor Law Movement |
| 1837 | Government implements new Poor Law in Bradford area at Court House, Hall Ings | 6 Metropolitan Police Officers sent to maintain order. Riot. 9 arrested |
| 1838 | Establishment of Northern Star Chartist Newspaper in Leeds | Editor – Fergus O'Connor |
| 1839 | Great Northern Union created. Bradford delegate sent to Convention | Call to arms and physical support speech made if moral force (presentation of the Charter) failed |
| 1839 | Radical meetings in and around Bradford | Much of class bitterness evident in the rise of Chartism in Bradford. Failure of Charter created a Chartist platform |
| 1840 | Economic depression. Rising of 26th June 1840 in Bradford | 9 people jailed |
| August 1841 | Fergus O'Connor released from York jail | Welcomed to Bradford by Bradford Chartists |

and drastic wage cuts in the factories, mills and coal mines. It also gave an opportunity for striking workers encouraged by the Chartist Movement to adopt some of the the political demands and principles espoused by Chartism.

These strikes which affected the Midlands, North of England and Scotland became known as the "Plug Plots" because striking workers removed the plugs from factory steam boilers and reservoirs to make factories inoperable. This was confrontation not only with employers, but also the State, thus from May 1842 more force was thrown against the authorities than any other year in the 19th Century. This involved nearly half a million workers and represented the biggest single exercise of working class strength in 19th Century Britain.

## Bradford Events

After a Chartist meeting on Bradford Moor on 14th August 1842 those attending were encouraged to march to Halifax to stop the mills there. On 15th August they did so stopping mills on their route through Odsal, Wibsey, Shelf and Northowarm. On their return via Queensbury and Great Horton they did similar, managing to close Ackroyd's Mill and Black Dyke Mills.

## Effects on Bingley

On 15th August a large body of 2000 men left Bradford to stop the mills at Shipley, Cottingley, Bingley, East Morton, Keighley, Denholme, Harden, Cullingworth, Haworth and Wilsden.

The local magistrates having heard of the likely agitation, displayed a poster in Bingley, reading:

*To the Inhabitants and Parishioners of Bingley. CAUTION. All peaceable and well disposed persons residing, or being in Bingley, are respectfully and earnestly requested to keep within Doors and not to join the deluded persons who are tumultuously assembling themselves together and perambulating the Manufacturing Districts for an unlawful purpose.*

*Signed – William Ellis, Edwin Greenwood, Rawdon Briggs, William Busfeild Ferrand, Magistrates.*

## Drawing of the Plugs

A report in the Bradford Observer of August 18th, gave the following account of what happened next:

*"Several thousand's left Bradford early on Tuesday and proceeded towards Shipley, where they stopped all the mills with the exception of the corn mill without difficulty, there being no protective force.*

*From there they marched on Bingley along the canal bank, and commenced their work of putting a stop to all business. A great augmentation took place when they proceeded in the direction of the large cotton factory belonging to William Ellis Esq of Castlefields situate on the banks of the River Aire. This gentleman had a large number of special constables sworn in, (he was one of the local Magistrates) but they proved of no avail.*

*The people here commenced by drawing the clews and letting off the water from the reservoirs: the clews were then destroyed and the water-wheel thrown out of gearing. After leaving this place, a detachment was sent from the main body to East Morton where several small factories were stopped; as also the paper manufactories of Messrs Smith and Messrs Clapham. At Harden, Cullingworth and Wilsden they stopped the mills before going on to Denholme.*

*The main body also proceeded to Cottingley at which place the mill of Messrs Ramsden and Co was stopped. Later at Stockbridge Toll Bar Keighley, which the keeper had locked, the Toll Bar was immediately broken open. Large numbers of people from Keighley joined the gathering and visited the different mills and stopped those that were not stopped by the owners."*

By the evening the mob had returned to Bradford and a military presence had kept the town relatively quiet. Despite some other activity at Stanningley, Bramley, Fulneck, Dudley Hill and Bowling on 17th August, by 20th August Bradford was again quiet. Magistrates informed the Home Office three days later that Town and District were quiet *"with all the mills now working again as well as most in the surrounding villages."* A number of arrests were made and rioters jailed, including two men who got six months imprisonment for plug drawing at Bingley.

Wright (1983) *The Chartist Risings in Bradford* comments that in the aftermath of the 1842 risings, Chartism in Bradford as elsewhere, went into decline.... for a time. He suggested that this may have been partly due to a mellowing of tone and flexibility by Government and the propertied classes and some sympathy with the starving workers. He also comments that there was a lack of a clear idea at both national and local level about what to do next, which caused further divisions within the Chartist Movement. See Chartism 1848 - Chelsea Pensioners Defend Bingley on pages 60 - 64 for the next development.

# Disraeli's Visit to Bingley and Druids Altar

**This Chapter looks at the background to a visit made to Bingley by Disraeli in 1844 and the reasons for his journey to the North of England.**

### Disraeli and Ferrand

In 1842 Benjamin Disraeli was one of the founder members of the Young England group which included W Busfeild Ferrand of Bingley. Disraeli was to be a future Prime Minister. Ferrand was a local squire and from 1841 to 1847 he was the MP for Knaresborough. He was an advocate of the 10 Hour Bill and a leading supporter of the Truck Act 1845.

### What was Young England?

Young England comprised of a group of four young conservative writers and politicians who argued that the middle classes were gaining too much economic and political power at the expense of the working classes. They believed that capitalists totally disregarded the needs of the working classes, and that the newly rich had no sense of obligation or duty.

Their rather vague and romantic ideology was that through a union of hearts and minds rather than specific social reforms, class peace and social stability could be restored. They proposed that to achieve this there needed to be a restoration of the trust which they believed had once existed between the aristocracy and the people, and a reaffirmation of the position of the church. Disraeli suggested that the aristocracy should use their power to protect the poor.

### Ferrands Position

Roberts (1979) *Paternalism in Early Victorian England* identifies that Ferrands Yorkshire was a centre of manufacturing which faced the dilemmas caused by old declining handcraft based industry, new technology and new and expanding textile mills. His speeches in public and in Parliament showed a bitter resentment at the excessive growth of manufacturing, the power of money and the focus on political economy.

In a speech to the House of Commons in March 1843 Ferrand used his powers of oratory in proposing Allotment of Waste Land as a means of redressing the perceptions and position of the working classes. In the speech he cited Bingley which he stated had once been a primarily agricultural centre with one manufacturer which had expanded in a short time to ten. He proposed that in granting land to the working class for their use as allotments *The measures which I am now about to propose would restore the working classes of the country in great degree to their former comforts."*

Eighteen months later in October 1844 he invited Young England colleagues Disraeli and Sir John Manners to Bingley to celebrate the success of the allotments which he had instituted.

### Bingley Allotments

On October 15th 1844 The Morning Chronicle gave background to the opening of new allotments on land owned by the Ferrands near Cottingley Bridge:

*"About twelve months ago Mr Ferrand introduced the allotment system into his parish. A field of about fifteen acres in extent, watered on two sides by the River Aire, was given by Mr Ferrands aunt for the purpose of ascertaining how far the system would prove serviceable to the poorer inhabitants of the parish, on condition that she continued to receive the accustomed rent.*

*The ground had been divided into 59 allotments and eleven shillings a year was charged to each allotment holder. The majority of these were operatives from worsted mills in Bingley and neighbourhood. Taking into account that rent and taxes collected raised £40 and cutting the grass cost £60, it was estimated that the crops produced amounted in value to between £400 and £500.*

Additionally, the article stated *"During the whole of the summer and autumn these 59 men and their families have been provided with good vegetables, many of them are keeping two pigs, while each allotment yields a good winter crop of potatoes."*

### The Local Environment

The town of Bingley was described as *"being the centre of the great*

51

*manufacturing workshops of Lancashire and Yorkshire, it is one of those places abounding in the North of England which exhibits the rapid and almost incredible change of an insignificant village into a vast manufacturing population."*

The article then continued in lyrical fashion, the writer obviously feeling the muse of the occasion in stating:

*"The town itself is beautifully placed on the river Aire in the midst of one of the most lovely dales in Yorkshire. Lofty and thickly wooded hills, a picturesque valley, mingled with the evidence of most active manufacturing industry, form a romantic and unusual scene. The tall chimneys as it were, appear to be struggling for mastery, with the luxuriant woods and to be shouldering them out of place, and the clinking of the power looms and spinning frames of the factories harmonise oddly with the free and joyous carol of the birds!"*

## The Allotment Opening and Celebration Dinner

On the afternoon of October 14th the townspeople of Bingley gathered at the cricket ground close to the allotments were they were met by Ferrand, Disraeli and Manners. In procession behind the town band they visited the allotments before returning to play a game of cricket on the ground that Ferrand had also given to them. The press of the time made great stock out of the fact that the Lord (Manners) and the local shoemaker had played together. Ferrands "locals" beat Manners XI by three games to two.

Those invited including representatives from agriculture, the factories, the allotment holders and local landowners and administrators (a target group of potential Young England supporters) who then walked to the Oddfellows Hall at the Ferrands Arms in Bingley. Dinner was served at four o clock and was followed by speeches.

A flag over the top table at the dinner carried the slogan "The Throne and the Cottages," the intention being to convey the idea of mutually supportive integrated relationship. This would entail the "aristocracy" (landed and industrial), providing security to their tenants and workers by supplying work and possibly housing care, which in turn would create loyalty amongst the workforce.

Disraeli took the opportunity to profile Young England ideology during his speech when he stated: *"We are on the eve of a big change which will bring back some of those ancient hereditary sentiments of loyalty and good faith and trust that once made England great (much cheering)* He also made reference to raising the tone of public feeling and that the dinner had been *"a genuine determination to blend classes together and restore the ancient feeling of good intelligence."* The similarity of Press Releases of the time and positive spin within them give evidence of a great degree of stage management of the event and those who were invited to attend.

## *Sybil* – Disraeli's Political Novel

Another reason for Disraeli's visit to the North was that he was writing and carrying out research for his second political novel *Sybil*. Whilst in the area he collected information about industrial life which he wrote up over the winter of 1844 and published in May 1845. In each of Disraeli's three novels the main characters were portrayed as showing concern about poverty and of the injustices of the parliamentary system

Blake (1966) in *Disraeli* points out that in *Sybil,* Disraeli gave a highly realistic picture of life in the grim northern manufacturing towns which formed the breeding ground of Chartism. This picture was based partly on his own observations, partly on the correspondence of Feargus O'Connor obtained for him by his friend Thomas Duncombe and very largely through his access as an MP to the"Blue Book" records of Parliamentary Committees and Royal Commissions.

## Druids Altar

During their visit to Bingley Disraeli and Manners stayed as guests of Ferrand at Harden Grange. Whilst they were there they visited Druids Altar, which left a marked impression on Disraeli. So much so that he used it as an important location for a torchlight meeting of revolutionary trade unionists in *Sybil*.

*"Suddenly in the distance the sound of martial music: and instantly, quick as the lighting and far more wild, each person present brandished a flaming torch, amid a chorus of cheers, that renewed and resounding floated far away over the broad bosom of the dusk wilderness.*

*The music and banners denoted the arrival of the leaders of the people. They mounted the craggy ascent to* **Druids Altar***, and there, surrounded by his companions, amid the enthusiastic shouts of the multitude, Walter Gerard came forward to address a torchlight meeting."*

Shortly after publication, Manners wrote to Disraeli on 11th May 1845 congratulating him on the book, which he had just finished reading. He

Druids Altar

also made reference to Harden Moor and Druids Altar. On 12th May 1845 Disraeli replied:

*"I was very pleased that you recognised the moor where we were companions. Do you remember your mounting the Druids Altar? Mrs Disraeli was frightened by your audacity. I think it gave me the idea for the Altar as Gerards rostrum."*

## Disraelis' Opinion of *Sybil*

After positive comment from Manners, Disraeli reflected on the book and what it represented, with pride as to its content and accuracy:

*"In Sybil, I considered the condition of the people. At that time the Chartist agitation was still fresh in the public memory, and its repetition was far from improbable. I had mentioned to my friend, the late Thomas Duncombe, something of what I was contemplating; and he offered and obtained for my perusal the whole of the correspondence of Feargus O'Connor when conductor of the Northern Star, with the leaders and chief actors of the Chartist movement.*

*I had visited and observed with care all the localities introduced ; and as an accurate and never exaggerated picture of a remarkable period in our domestic history, and of a popular organisation which in its extent and completeness has perhaps never been equalled, the pages of Sybil may, I venture to believe, be consulted with confidence."*

## Postscript to the Visit To Bingley

Despite the rhetoric, Young England ceased to exist as a political group in 1845 partly owing to differences in opinion on government proposals and partly because of pressure on two of the group, not to be disloyal to their main party. As a literary circle they ceased to exist in 1848.

Although no longer connected as a political alliance, Ferrand and Disraeli continued to correspond. In a letter dated 27th August 1854 Disraeli remembers his trip to Bingley.

*"My Dear Ferrand,*
*Hearty thanks for your ever kind recollection of us. I have an especial relish for your Harden Grouse which always reminds me of the old moor, and the happy visit we paid in 1844. Is it possible that 10 years can have passed?"*

The real postscript to this chapter is that whilst Ferrand, Disraeli and Young England may be distant memories, the Bingley and Cottingley Allotments which they helped institute are still a much used local facility 167 years later.

# Railway Comes to Bingley

This Chapter traces the advent of the railway system through Bingley and the positive effects which are still being appreciated in the town.

## Dominance of the Railways

With the development of rail transport in the 19th century, canals declined as the dominant carriers of freight. Eventually, canals could not compete with rail as they were limited both in the volume carried per unit and in speed. In contrast, the railways, as they became integrated into national systems, provided a far more extensive service with greater flexibility. They exploited the difficulties of the canals by drastic rate cutting that forced many canal companies to sell out to them. By the 1840's and 50's a third of the canals became railway-owned.

*Original Station below Three Rise Locks*

## Local Background

In July 1843 an Act of Parliament was passed, to build a line from Wellington Street, Leeds, to Bradford via Shipley; and also a link to the North Midlands terminus at Hunslet Lane, to allow connections to the south. The engineer in charge of the project was George Stephenson. The passing of the Leeds and Bradford (Shipley to Keighley) Extension

Railway Act of 30th June 1845 allowed the building of a line as an extension to the Leeds and Bradford Railway.

Work on the seven mile line started in June 1846 and was completed in nine months, the statistics of the build being impressive...... including the removal of 150,000 cubic yards of earth and rock near Shipley Station, digging out of 70,000 cubic yards of earth to build a cutting at Hirst Wood, the construction of a 250 foot long wooden bridge over the river Aire and a stone viaduct of three arches at Dowley Gap, and the building of a stone tunnel 250 yards in length beneath Bingley on the approach to Bingley Station.

## Bingley Bog

The bottom of the valley at Bingley was originally a large glacial lake linked historically to the existence of a north bog and a south bog which determined the placing of the early road, canal and railway systems in Bingley. The contractors of the Bingley Relief Road (2003) also met with many of the problems encountered by their earlier counterparts.

As regards the building of the railway, Speight (1899) *Chronicles of Old Bingley* records "*the problems of filling up of the terrible Bingley Bog to which more than 100,0000 cubic yards, chiefly of stone and gravel had to be tipped into . This apparently "bottomless marsh" was the greatest difficulty which the contractors Messrs George Thompson and Co had to contend with in the whole course of the railway.... at one time it was thought the idea of traversing the valley at this point would have to be abandoned and the line carried along the side of the valley like the canal contractors had done.*"

## The Directors Inspection

Eventually the problems of the bog were overcome by placing the railway track on an embankment to one side of the valley. At 2.20 on the afternoon of March 13th 1847 Captain Simmons, the Government Railway Inspector and Directors of the Railway Company accompanied by the Contracting Engineers set out from Shipley Station to inspect the full length of the track to Keighley. The train was a small one, consisting of the engine Camilla and three carriages. An article in the Halifax, Huddersfield and Keighley Reporter records the entire journey, crowds, weather, landmarks passed and excitement of the forty minute journey. This article can be accessed through the Local Studies section of Bradford Libraries at Keighley.

The article also records that Keighley Station was sited close to the Keighley and Bradford Turnpike Road. This link to previous transport systems is also captured by an advertisement in the Bradford and Wakefield Observer March 18th 1847 which besides giving train times, states "All the above trains stop at Bingley. – Coaches from Keighley to Skipton, Colne and Kendal. This reference suggests that stage-coaches continued to operate on some routes.

*1847 Newspaper advertisement for the railway*

## The Opening of the Shipley to Keighley line

The line from Shipley to Keighley was opened for passenger traffic on 16th March 1847 on what the Leeds Mercury reported as "*A most auspicious day, the sun shone in unclouded brilliance during the greater part of the day. Eight trains ran from Leeds , Bradford and Keighley respectively during the course of the day, most of which carried a large number of passengers.*" Bingley Station at this time existed as a wooden structure and a station house.

*The original station*

## Bingley Station

Speight (1899) writing about the Directors Inspection states" *"never has such a cheer been heard in Bingley since the lowering of the first canal boat down the five rise locks seventy years before, as old folks tell me went forth from at least 3000 throats on that memorable day when the train drew up for a few minutes at Bingley station which was then near Park Road corner, not far from the present station. The latter was opened July 24th 1892."*

New station

## 2011

The railway links between Leeds, Bradford, Skipton and beyond have stood the test of time and 164 years after opening, Bingley Station supports a growing commuter population as do other stations on the network. The station buildings have changed little since 1892 with the horse transport once evident on the station forecourt having been replaced by different forms of horsepower.

## Past and Present

The origins of transport through Bingley owe much to the geography and shape of the valley in which Bingley is set. The communications networks needed to support the expansion of industry in the area also had a major influence from the 1600's up to the late 1900's.

Nowadays, in a compact space across the width of the valley bottom at Bingley lie the River Aire, A591 ( a former turnpike and coaching road), the railway, Bingley Relief Road and the Leeds to Liverpool canal. How many localities the size of Bingley can claim the close proximity between such a range of historical and current transport links some of which have been around for almost 300 years?

# Chartism – Chelsea Pensioners Defend Bingley?

This Chapter picks up the story of the Chartists final attempt at presenting a third Charter to Parliament and the confrontations arising at local level.

## Chartism Nationally

In 1847 Feargus O'Connor, now the Chartist leader and figurehead was elected to Parliament, the only Chartist ever to become an MP.

The last occasion on which the Chartists offered a direct challenge to authority was in 1848 following a winter of economic recession. As news was received from Europe of revolutions in France and Italy in the early Spring of 1848, the Chartists began to organise a third Petition. Elaborate precautions were taken by the authorities everywhere against a possible rising, including control of the new telegraph and railway systems. Troops were strategically placed at locations near to railway stations, ready to respond within hours of trouble breaking out.

The Chartist Convention arranged a mass rally on Kennington Common, London to be followed by a procession to the House of Commons with the third petition. The rally attracted far fewer than O'Connor had hoped for and additionally the authorities banned the procession to Parliament. In the end O'Connor presented the Petition alone. When examined by the authorities it contained a large number of forged entries and less signatures than had been claimed, which in essence led to the Charter being rejected for a third time. This did little or nothing to aid the Chartist cause.

Plans for further protest and violence amounted to little and were mostly concentrated in the North. By midsummer, most advocates of force in the North were under arrest.

## Ferrand and Bingley

One one hand Ferrand was appalled by the inhumanity of the factory system and he actively campaigned to support reform of "infant slavery" and the introduction of the 10 Hour Factory Bill and the 1847 Factory Act.

He was however as an establishment figure and magistrate vehemently opposed to the thought of revolution against the state or the notion of insurgency. Two events occurred locally in 1848 which caused him major concern.

- A Chartist camp meeting on Bingley Moor on 26 March attracted some 5,000 people. Banners bearing the colours of the French Republic were carried in procession, and there were reports of speakers urging the crowd to arm themselves.

- A local demonstration on 24 May in Bingley which led to what became known as the Little Siege of Bingley, the main characters being:

Ferrand, Thomas Kilvington a weaver, William Smith a fishmonger, Thomas Bland a shopkeeper, and Isaac Ickeringill a mill operative.

### Drilling and Marching

On Wednesday 24 May 1848 about 100 men assembled in Myrtle Place Bingley for the purpose of drilling and marching. At their head, local men Thomas Kilvington and William Smith acted as drill sergeants to the group who were reported to be dressed in military attire, carrying banners and flags, some of which were reported to be the French Tricolour and parading with a band.

Myrtle Place, Bingley, 1848.

A warrant for their arrest was issued against them and on Friday 26th May 1848 shortly before 5pm they appeared in front of Ferrand in the justice room at the Brown Cow Inn, Bingley where they were charged with illegal training, drilling and practising military movements.

Five local constables and two special constables were asked by the Magistrate to escort the two prisoners to Bingley railway station to catch the 5.48pm train en route for York. Once there they were to be imprisoned at York Castle awaiting trial by jury.

## Bail?

However, local Chartists and friends of the prisoners had other ideas and a large crowd assembled and followed the constables towards the railway station. At Fowles Yard, about 150 yards from the station the crowd stopped the constables and several people including Thomas Bland a Special Constable who was part of the crowd, offered to be bail for the prisoners. A stone was thrown, injuring one of the constables who threatened by the behaviour of some of the crowd and perhaps thinking that bail should be considered returned with their captives to the Brown Cow.

*Brown Cow*

At first Magistrate Ferrand intimated his willingness to accept bail on the basis of four sureties at £25 or two at £50. Thomas Bland offered himself and was accepted as surety. Other sureties were then sought. Over a period of three quarters of an hour, the mood of all involved became more heated. Ickeringill stood on a bench and in addressing Ferrand and the crowd complained about Kilvington and Smith being apprehended as the law seemed to be unjust and class made. He asserted that there was one law for the rich and another for the poor.

Ferrand in response said that he was a friend of the poor and in favour of small allotments of land (a reference to his support for the setting up of allotments in Bingley in 1843). Later at the court hearings he would claim that he had begged the crowd not to rescue the two prisoners as the consequences would be bad to themselves.

## Rescue

Due to delays, the crowd now numbering around 200 became impatient and forced their way into the justice room and succeeded in rescuing both prisoners. Kilvington and Smith had both been handcuffed, so the mob took them over Ireland Bridge to Lambert's blacksmiths opposite the White Horse Inn to have the shackles hammered and filed off. After this the men were paraded through the town.

## Threats

Several incidents then happened which escalated the seriousness of the situation. Reports of these inferred that Ferrand had been threatened with his life and that some of the moors near his home had been set on fire as a warning to him. The Magistrates Clerk was also threatened and held over the parapet of Ireland Bridge to frighten him. A boat, the Water Witch, owned by one of the constables was also set on fire and destroyed.

Feelings ran high locally and there were many in Bingley who either secretly or openly supported or aided "the insurgents." A comment in the Northern Echo of June 7th 1848 captures the atmosphere in stating *"There was not a Special Constable in the town who would act until the military were called in."*

## Military Action including the Chelsea Pensioners!

In the event, on the following Wednesday, 31st May 1848 at 7am sixty soldiers from the 52nd Regiment of Infantry supported by sixty six Chelsea Pensioners sent from London by train, took up their positions in and around Bingley. At about the same time two troops of Yorkshire Hussars marched into the town from Otley and took up positions on approaches to the town and to the railway station. The Keighley Road near Crossflatts, Cottingley Bridge and Park Road Bridge plus the station itself were all closely guarded.

The reason for the presence of the soldiers was to assist the civil authorities in arresting men who had been identified as either assisting the escape of Kilvington and Smith on the previous Friday, or to have taken part in drilling the previous Wednesday.

In less than an hour 16 men had been arrested either at work in the mills or at home and were brought by local constables and the Chelsea Pensioners to the station. Here a special train was waiting to take them to York Castle and the prisoners were handcuffed and chained to the carriages and the constables were issued with loaded pistols.

The Chelsea Pensioners came in for some ridicule locally as is identified in the following statement from the Northern Star of June 10th 1848.

*"Each (Pensioner) carried a gun and sixty rounds of ball cartridge and the appearance of the motley crew of old men, like the fag-end of Falstaffs regiment of all sorts and sizes appeared to excite a good deal of curiosity."* Speight (1898) *Old Bingley* records *"The pensioners were armed with old flint-lock blunderbusses.... they were all more or less fully armed, though considerable doubt was expressed as to whether half the old matchlocks would really go off properly if required. The men had to put up with a great deal of joking."*

*Victorian Chelsea Pensioners*

At the jury trial in York on July 26th 1848 the following sentences were passed:

Issac Ickeringill, Joseph Hollings (or Hallings), Thomas Bottomley, H.Rawsthorne, T.Whitaker, E.Lee, J.Crabtree, J.Taylor, W.Smith, R.Atkinson, John Quinn *"captured in the mills, while at work, for assisting in the rescue of T.Kilvington and W.Smith."* Sent by special train to York castle. Later discharged on surety of £50 to keep the peace. mith sentenced to 18 months with hard labour, Ickeringill sentenced to six months with hard labour, Crabtree to two months, Kilvington to one month; J.Bland, a special constable, fined £10 for neglect of duty.

After 1848 Chartism lost its mass support. It then became a movement promoting education, temperance, cooperative effort, municipal reforms, and settlement on the land—whilst never losing faith that universal suffrage would someday, somehow, be won which it eventually was. Of the six points of the Charter, all were eventually achieved with the exception of an Annual Parliament.

# The Influence of William Morris and the Pre Raphaelite Movement In Harden, Bingley and Silsden

## Background to Morris and the Pre Raphaelites

What, you may ask, had the industrial areas of the Aire Valley to do with the Pre-Raphaelites? The district was in fact a pioneer in recognizing the merits of **William Morris** and his ideas and as such a number of local benefactors were at the forefront of being early supporters of the firm of Morris, Marshall, Faulkner and Co which was founded in 1861. Leach and Pevsner (2009) *The Buildings of England –West Yorkshire* state *"During the 1860's Bingley was for a short time an example of the artistically innovative with work by Norman Shaw, Morris and Co and William Burges amongst others."*

### A National Perspective

*William Burges*

William Morris was one of the most significant voices in Victorian art and architecture, and his influence also helped shape the Arts and Crafts Movement of the 20th Century

In 1859 Morris commissioned a friend Philip Webb, to design a new home for him called The, Red House in Bexley Heath. The house was to be built in a simple style using traditional materials. Morris found it difficult to find good internal decoration, textiles and furniture to suit this philosophy, so he decided to design them himself. With the help of friends including **Edward Burne-Jones, Dante Gabriel Rossetti**, Ford Maddox Brown and Webb he did so, later forming a small firm, eventually called Morris and Company, to sell the products they designed. **William Burges** was an early visitor to Morris's Red House in the summer of 1861.

Behind Morris' designing there was a profound social philosophy. He was a committed socialist and medievalist who was horrified by increasing mechanization and mass-production in the arts. His dream was to re-establish the values of traditional craftsmanship and simplicity of design.

Under Morris' leadership the company soon made a name for itself as a high quality producer of stained glass, furniture, wallpaper and textiles. The firm's medieval inspired ethic and respect for hand crafts and traditional textile arts had a major influence on the decoration of houses and churches which carried over into the 20th Century.

*So where does the Aire Valley fit in?*

## A Local Perspective

The mid 1800's and effects of industrialisation saw a move away from control by a local "Squirearchy" based on land ownership and inheritance, to a "network of influence" formed by new money and created by the expansion of the local manufacturing base and industrialisation.

Local manufacturers became involved in church and local business and political affairs as well as seeing themselves as patrons of the arts as regards building, furnishing or decorating their new or refurbished large houses. To an extent evidence suggests that a philosophy of "keeping up with the Jones's also existed amongst these "benefactors".

In researching this chapter I became aware that many of the sources used made mention of one individual Pre Raphaelite application locally rather than seeking to make links with others. In the chapter I will **highlight** in bold those names and places which are **common denominators** potentially linking with each other.

I have identified religious buildings in Bingley and Bradford and houses in Harden, Bingley and Silsden. For the purposes of this chapter I will concentrate on those buildings which had Pre Raphaelite connections between 1860 and the early 1870's.

*Burne Jones and Morris 1890*

*Rossetti*

## Woodbank – Harden

John Aldam Heaton a manufacturer at Beehive Mill in Bradford moved to Woodbank an ancient farm near Harden in May 1860 (Speight 1898 *Old Bingley*). He followed an interest in designing furniture, stained glass and wallpaper and was strongly influenced by the Pre Raphaelite movement. He was one of the first in this district to recognise the merits of the work of Morris and his friends. The *Holy Trinity Church Centenary Brochure 1868 – 1968*

*Drawing Room Windows, Woodbank, 1936*

establishes *"Amongst Aldam Heatons friends were Rossetti, Burne-Jones, William Morris, and Norman Shaw. It is significant that examples of work by all these men are found in Bingley."*

Heaton invited **Rossetti** to stay at Woodbank to paint a portrait of Mrs Heaton which was eventually commissioned as a stained glass window for the house. In a letter to Heaton, in October 1861, Rossetti says *"I could spare a fortnight which, with hard work on my part and kind abundance on Mrs Heaton's, would suffice to do the portrait if not finish the picture"* In the event Rossetti stayed for a month between November and December 1861. Lawson (1985) *The Bradford Antiquary Volume 1*, Third Series; records that this must have been amongst the first products of the Morris studio.

In 1862 Heaton had a hand in recommending the Bradford Architects **Knowles and Wilcock** and the Morris Company to a textile manufacturer, **Walter Dunlop** who leased **Harden Grange** in that year.

Heaton in making recommendations was extremely confident of the quality of Morris's work. This matches a statement by Rossetti in January 1862 *"Our stained glass may challenge any other firm to approach it"* In 1863 Heaton suggested that the commission for glass at Bradford Cathedral and the design of a memorial window dedicated to a friend of his should be awarded to the company, even though this was said to be only their third commission. This was carried out as was subsequent work for the Cathedral.

Aldam Heaton is attributed by The Stained Glass Museum, Ely as probably having designed a Star of David window for **Holy Trinity Church Bingley** in the early 1870's.

Heaton left Harden to set up his own business in London as an artistic decorator. As his business developed he worked in collaborative partnership with **Richard Norman Shaw** an architect who besides having a national profile, carried out commissions at **Bingley Holy Trinity Church** and at **Silsden House**. Amongst work which Heaton did during his later career was the design and decoration of the State Rooms of the Titanic.

### Harden Grange

In 1862 **Walter Dunlop** made a number of additions to Harden Grange including building a music room and an entrance hall and staircase to showcase Morris glass. Morris provided Dunlop with a programme for the work entitled "Short abstract of the romance of Tristram"

The theme of the 13 small stained glass windows was built around the story of Sir Tristram and la Belle Isoude. Morris commissioned four of the artists who had previously worked with him on another Arthurian legend project, to design the cartoons and drawings for the 13 panels. Morris himself designed four of the panels with others being designed by **Burne –Jones, Rossetti**, Madox Brown and Val Prinsep.

Dunlop worshipped at Bingley All Saints Church and paid for the purchase of two bells which made a new peal of eight bells at the church.

In 1917 the Tristram and Isoude windows and the short abstract were acquired by Bradford Art Gallery.

### Silsden House

Records at the Stained Glass Museum show that in 1863 **Rossetti** designed a series of stained-glass panels for **Charles Hastings** a Bradford Worsted Spinning Manufacturer, for his house in Silsden.

They depicted the twelve Labours of the Months and were part of the décor of the house, designed by the architect **Norman Shaw**.

Whilst a sketch design (March – A Woodcutter) and two of the panels

(August – Threshing and December – Killing a Hog) still exist in the William Morris Gallery at Walthamstow, the others remain untraced. It is however known that the glass was removed before the house was demolished in 1903.

Evidence that there was a Pre Raphaelite connection with the house is shown in the notice of sale of the house in the Leeds Mercury of March 6th 1888:

*Richard Norman Shaw*

*"Mr William Lawson, Auctioneer, Bradford Begs to announce that he has received instructions to sell by auction the residence of Mr Charles Hastings, Silsden House, Silsden.*

*"The Choice and elegant contents of the above Country Mansion are all of fine quality, style and design and in excellent condition. The lots include the tastefully designed appointments of dining room and drawing room suites from the designs of R Norman Shaw, William Morris and others.*

*Omnibuses meet every train from Bradford and will take passengers up to the house."*

**Aldam Heaton** and **Charles Hastings** were in partnership together during the 1860's as Commission Agents. The London Gazette of 7 January 1868 announced that this partnership had been dissolved.

### Oakwood Hall

In 1864 a recently married **Thomas Garnett** co-founder of Gillies Garnett Stuff Merchants, commissioned architects **Knowles and Wilcox** to design a new gothic villa for him in Bingley, called Oakwood Hall.

Taylor and Symondson (*Architectural Review* July 1968) *Burges and Morris at Bingley – A Discovery* identify that for advice on the interior decoration for his new home, Garnett turned to his cousin Charles Beanlands (born in Bingley) who was founder vicar of St Michael's Church, Brighton. Beanlands had also been the presiding vicar at Garnett's wedding in Scarborough. He also had experience of the work of **Burges** and **Morris** who had designed a series of windows and furnishings for his new church at Brighton and was consequently happy to recommend them and their fellow artists to Garnett.

On receiving the commission William Burges contacted the architects and prepared *Detail Drawings of Furniture etc for Thomas Garnett, Oakwood, Bingley, Designed by William Burges, Architect*. This showed architects plans of the building, furniture, layout, ceilings, wall panels and fireplaces in the lounge and dining room and is now held in the RIBA Collection at the Victoria and Albert Museum. Having viewed it as part of my research, it captures the Pre Raphaelite style of Burges in terms of the colour, style and flair which he is suggesting to Garnett.

Notable amongst the watercolour drawings are two fireplaces. Whilst one no longer exists, the other carved by **Thomas Nicholls** with letters TG in a shield signifying the owners name, and surmounted by a Lincoln Imp, is still resplendent in what is now the bar of the Oakwood Hall Hotel. The ceiling in this room is also the original designed by Knowles and Wilcox.

Morris and **Burne-Jones** are attributed with the design of the stained glass windows at the top of the stairs on the first floor landing above the entrance. These show St George flanked by female figures of the Four Seasons as well as depicting Chaucer flanked by the heads of four female

*Fireplace, Oakwood Hall Hotel*

*Morris and Burne-Jones windows, Oakwood Hall Hotel*

Chaucerian Heroines. A white rose and red rose are also included on two upper lights indicating that the Garnett family lived in both Yorkshire and Lancashire.

Garnett and his wife died within a few days of each other in 1916. His eldest son Harold sold Oakwood and moved presumably with any Burges furniture into White Lodge the former vicarage of **Holy Trinity Church**, Bingley. I have managed to trace a card table described in Burges' Detail Drawings to the Minneapolis Institute of Arts but apart from this it has not been possible to trace any further Burges furniture.

Whilst Garnett and his family were initially regular worshippers at **Bingley All Saints Church**, records show that from the 1870's they

71

transferred to Holy Trinity Church. An article in the Keighley News in May 1912 states *"Mr and Mrs Garnett have always been amongst the best supporters of Holy Trinity Church and the interests of the church and school have always held a warm place in their hearts."*

## Bingley All Saints Church

In 1870 **Norman Shaw** carried out restoration of the north chapel. In 1873 a memorial window to four children who died in infancy was designed by **Burne-Jones** and erected as the north chancel chapel window of the church. The three panels illustrated Angels playing long trumpets.

## Holy Trinity Church

In 1874 a twenty two feet six inches by four feet six stained glass window attributed to **Burne-Jones** and **Morris** was installed in the east window of the church. The upper part depicted a large crucifix and the lower, the Crucifixion and Sacrifice of Isaac. The church was demolished in 1974 and glass from the windows was acquired by Bradford Museums and Galleries. Design of the church, school and vicars residence is attributed to Norman Shaw.

*Burne-Jones and Morris window, Holy Trinity Church*

## Local Networks

My research has highlighted the possible direct and indirect links between the Pre Raphaelite sponsors in the local area, mainly through church contacts. Advertisements in the Leeds Mercury of the time also show that Dunlop, Garnett, Hastings and Aldam Heaton were all General Committee members of the Bradford arm of the British Association for the Advancement of Science, who would have come into contact with each other on a regular basis in business terms.

## Morris and the Pre Raphaelites Networks

The members of Morris's artistic and architectural network obviously exchanged information on commissions with each other. What is also apparent is the link to architects such as Norman Shaw and sculptors like Thomas Nicholls and the use of local architects Knowles and Wilcox.

In later life Morris became a founder of the Socialist League and visited Keighley and Bingley to espouse his socialist beliefs.

## Morris' Dilemma

Whilst politically he was a committed socialist, artistically it seems ironic that his ideal of "by the people, for the people" was at odds with the fact that initially only those with considerable wealth or sponsorship could afford the fruits of his and his colleagues artistic endeavours!

## And Finally...........

Between 1870 and 1873 work began on building perhaps the most Gothic of all the large houses in the local area. **Milner Field** designed by architect Thomas Harris and built for Titus Salt Junior as a home for his family also had Pre Raphaelite connections..... but more of Milner Field on page 84.

# The Mechanics Institute – Bingley

This Chapter poses the question - Is the Mechanics Institute the oldest and most utilised building on Bingley Main Street? If so what were the different uses?

*Mechanics Institute, Main Street Bingley*

## Further Education and a Girls School

In 1864 the Mechanics Institute was erected in Main Street, Bingley by public subscription. Its purpose was to provide a venue for self-help classes and educational opportunities for working people. As such Mechanics Institutes were pioneers in further education, established to further understanding of technical and scientific subjects through a lecture and night school approach.

## The Leeds Mercury of 15th November 1864 reported that facilities included:

- A hall for lectures and music on the top floor which was designed to accommodate 500 people on the top floor
- A news reading room and classrooms on the ground floor
- A spacious schoolroom for elementary instruction and evening classes in the basement

In its first year in the new building, the Institute had 350 members and the reading room supplied seven daily and seven weekly newspapers. As a small library it also issued over 6000 books.

The clock to the Institute was initially the subject of some derision: its primary motive power was water which proved ineffective and for some time the clock was permanently stopped at a quarter to one until a new power supply was fitted in 1868.

From 1873 to 1879 a Girls School was carried on in the Mechanics Institute as a precursor to later integration with other schools in the area. (Dodd (1930) *History of the Bingley Grammar School).*

## Town Hall and Free Library

In 1890 the Mechanics Institute was leased as the Town Hall for Bingley and in 1892 the old reading and news room was converted into a Council Chamber. At a meeting of local ratepayers in 1890, the concept of the Free Libraries Act was adopted and accordingly a library was also opened in the building in 1892. This was supported by local benefactor Alfred Sharp of Myrtle Grove who contributed £1000 towards the purchase of new books.

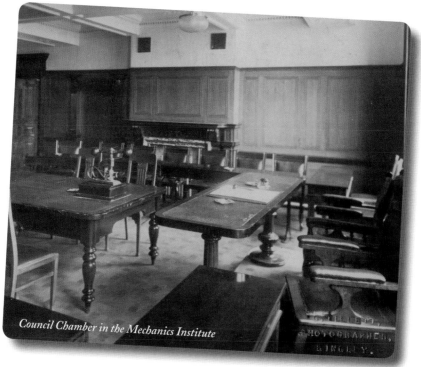

*Council Chamber in the Mechanics Institute*

## Public Baths

Around this time, sanitation and cleanliness were a major topic of debate at both national and local level. As a result, Bingley adopted the idea of public baths (not yet swimming baths, which were not built in Bingley until 1927).

The Leeds Mercury of March 12th 1892 reported:

*"The erection of public baths at Bingley Town Hall is almost completed. There is a Turkish Bath and two first class and five second class slipper baths, each fitted with arrangements for rapid filling and fed by a large cistern for hot water."*

The arrangements for the different aspects of the Institute to coexist together were:

- The basement was converted to Public Baths
- The ground floor became Public Offices
- The first floor became the Free Library

*1897 Diamond Jubilee of Queen Victoria*

## Workers Education Association

Bingley Urban District Council obtained the freehold to the building in 1907. Whilst the original function of the Mechanics Institute was the provision of general educational opportunities for workers, this was superseded by provision by the Workers Education Council, a branch of which was launched in Bingley in 1913. In the years immediately after First World War, the WEA flourished and the Bingley Branch based at the Mechanics Institute, was thought to be one of the most successful in the county in proportion to head of population.

## Public Library

After the adoption of "open access" in November 1923 and the awarding of a grant by the Carnegie Trust, the Public Library in Bingley steadily increased its services, whilst WEA influence sadly declined. The library also joined the Yorkshire Regional Library which made it possible to borrow books not included in local stock.

In 1926 the whole building of the Mechanics Institute was handed over to the Library and Myrtle Grove now became the Town Hall. 1928 saw the lending library and reading room being enlarged. The next major refurbishment was in 1946 when large scale alterations were carried out.

In 1950 an exhibition room was provided to house the model steam engine collection donated by Mr W H Smith and a Junior Library was opened in the former exhibition room. During 1960 a mobile library service was inaugurated to replace centres at Harden, Wilsden and Cullingworth. This service also covered Cottingley.

In March 1973 the former Mechanics Institute closed after 109 years, 81 of these as a Library. The reason for the closure was that the building was no longer fit for purpose as an expanding library.

## 1973 to 2011

The rest as they say....is history.

On 17th April 1973 the new central Library opened in the Myrtle Walk Shopping Centre where it remained until its relocation within the 5Rise Shopping Precinct opened in 2009.

When the Mechanics Institute was opened on Main Street in 1864 the dignitary who opened it prophesied:

*"It is a most beautiful building which will be an adornment to the town: it will enable the inhabitants to hold public meetings and to listen to lectures: for many, many years to come it will be destined that there will be much to instruct and please within these walls."*

147 years later the building still stands in a prominent position on Main Street having more than fulfilled its promise to instruct by serving the town at different times as a Mechanics Institute, Girls School, Town Hall/Council Chamber and Library. Nowadays it fulfils its promise to please by housing a Wine Bar and Dance School.

# The Bingley Boiler Explosion

Work was progressing as usual at Towns Bobbin Turners opposite Bingley Railway Station on Wednesday 9th June 1869. John Town and his brother Joseph had moved their business from Victoria Mills, Keighley to a two storey building in Bingley only three weeks before. Attached to their new premises were three cottages and a boiler house, the boiler of which had been in-situ for three years.

Across the street was the National School where children from the infants class were playing happily in the playground unaware of what was about to happen..

*National School and playground*

## Massive Blast

Suddenly and without warning, a massive explosion sent masonry, machinery, steam and dust into the air. Within seconds, the bobbin mill (with the exception of a portion of the south gable end wall) had been levelled to the ground and the playground opposite had taken the full brunt of scalding steam, falling masonry and rubble.

The Leeds Mercury of 10th June 1869 reported: *"At 10.30 am the boiler at the mill burst with a terrific boom killing 13 people on the spot. The explosion which in the adjoining school had more the effect of an earthquake was heard from a great distance, as the reverberation echoed from hillside to hillside through the valley of the Aire, which at this point is not of great breadth."*

The Glasgow Herald of the same date observed: "*Those who were witness of the scene from the Railway Station and the houses lying further up the slope on which the mill was built, heard first a loud report, accompanied by a rapid violent shaking of the earth and at the same instant there arose from the site a great cloud of dirty steam through which several masses of material were flying.*"

The falling ruin of the mill had been projected far into the infants playground where some of the younger children had been at play.

Eight children were killed instantly, the youngest being three and the eldest, seven. Five employees from the mill were killed, including the wife and young daughter of Joseph Town. Joseph himself was to die later as was Robert Hodgkinson the engine tenter in charge of the boiler.

Local people at the site of the explosion

## Police and Medical Help

A Superintendant Gill and a small number of policemen had at the time of the explosion been at the Petty Sessions at the Courthouse in Myrtle Place about 150 yards away. They were able to get to the site immediately to maintain order and assist in the search.

Dr Ruff, a surgeon and Dr Glendenning of Bingley were also immediately on site and were able to contact doctors from Shipley and Bradford by telegraph to assist them and the 33 injured in the aftermath of the explosion. The rooms at the school served a double purpose as a temporary hospital and mortuary.

## Violence of the Explosion

So violent was the blast that some of the bricks from the works chimney were hurled about 300 yards into the heart of the town. A 16 lb weight attached to the boiler safety valve was found near to the Fleece Inn 200 yards away and a large iron bolt was embedded in the railway embankment. The boiler was lifted from its seat by the explosion and landed in a "shapeless mass" forty yards away.

## The Aftermath

### Funds Appeal

Immediately a Committee was organised to help those affected directly by the disaster and collection boxes were placed in prominent positions throughout Bingley and on Park Road near the site of the explosion. Collections were taken in all the local churches and services were held for the bereaved. Visiting Church officials from a variety of denominations carried out impromptu prayer services at the site.

Four photographers were selected to take pictures of the site and the following advertisement appeared in newspapers throughout the UK:

---

**B**OILER EXPLOSION, BINGLEY. — VIEWS
of these RUINS may be had at the following prices :—
Cartes de Visite, 6d ; Stereoscopic, 1s. ; large size for framing, 2s. 6d. Postage 1d. each. Proceeds to be given for the relief of the poor families who have suffered by the accident. Application by post to B. LOWE, Photographer, Ilkley ; or to T. M. BURNS, Hill Street, Bingley.

---

Over the next month Committees in Bingley, Keighley and Haworth would raise over £1000 to help pay for funerals and care of the injured.

### Curiosity of the Victorians

The Bradford Observer of 14th June reported a huge influx of visitors to Bingley to view the accident site:

*"A larger number of persons have visited Bingley today (Sunday 13th June) than in all probability were ever seen there on any former occasion in its history.*

*They began to arrive with the early dawn and continued to pour into the town until sundown. The high roads from Bradford and Keighley, the by roads over the hills, the field paths, the canal bank and river side were alive with pedestrians. Conveyances of all kinds thronged the roads, from the largest omnibuses down to velocipedes, and even the canal boats were heavily freighted with passengers. The traffic on the Midland Railway was enormous and there was standing room only on trains."*

*Visitors at the site of the explosion*

## The Inquest

The first inquest took place on 11th June and the jury included Thomas Garnett of Oakwood Hall, Bingley and John Adlam Heaton of Woodbank, Harden, both manufacturers.

The jury formed the opinion that *"No boiler properly constructed at first, properly inspected from time to time and worked under proper supervision ought ever to burst."*

Evidence heard from a number of inquest witnesses gave rise to speculation about the condition of the boiler, namely:

- That it was fired up to too high a pressure
- The boiler overheated.
- The whistle on the safety steam valve had been tied up and alarm whistle muzzled
- A weak plate had been forced to give way by the pressure

81

After viewing and examining fragments of the shattered boiler the jury requested the Coroner to *"call on the services of an independent and well qualified engineer to advise them on the subject."*

## The Engineers Report

The Engineer selected was Mr L E Fletcher who was Chief Engineer of the Steam Users Association whose report and the Coroners comments concluded:

*"The boiler which exploded was not ill-shaped, and that is about all the good that can be said of it. Boilers are of various "types" or patterns, and the Bingley boiler was of the type commonly employed in the Lancashire and Yorkshire mills. So far, but no further, was the inquiry satisfactory; every step beyond appears to have disclosed something wrong.*

*The boiler was never a good one, to begin with, having been constructed of inferior material. The plates of which it was composed were not of the quality desirable in boiler plates, but were suitable only for the manufacture of water tanks or other such purposes.*

*Moreover, such as it was it was not new, having been bought second-hand. It had been worked in another establishment for some eight or nine years, when it was taken out, purchased by a boiler-maker, repaired, and resold. At that time it was found to be wasted at the bottom by external corrosion, and the worn parts were cut away and re-placed by new plates, but not sufficiently or with proper skill. The repairs were not carried far enough, the new plates, nearly half an inch thick, being riveted on to old plates which had worn away to a quarter of an inch, and thus lost half their original strength.*

*With much likelihood does the Report proceed to tell us that it is "difficult to make good " work in this way, and on the present occasion the work was certainly anything but good. The machine thus tinkered up lasted just three years, and the only wonder is how it could have endured so long. An examination of the fragments showed that leakage had soon begun at the junction of the old work and the new, so that in more than one place the plates had been reduced " to the thickness of a sheet of paper." It was through these places that the rent had started, which ended in the destruction of the boiler.*

*The boiler, besides the defects of its material, was ill "equipped" also. When it changed owners, its safety-valve was altered, and the valve actually in use was too small and of bad construction.*

*To complete the tale of faults, the engine-tenter in charge of the boiler is supposed to have been both incompetent and reckless, and to have kept up an excessive pressure of steam. As regards this point, however, Mr. Fletcher was of the opinion that "some more practical lesson should be drawn from this "fatal catastrophe than to throw the onus of fifteen deaths upon an ignorant stoker already killed by the explosion."*

## The Verdict

The Inquest Jury found the Robert Hodkinson the engine tenter was guilty of manslaughter and that the greatest possible blame attached to the Messrs Town, the occupiers of a mill in which a manifestly incompetent engine tenter was employed and in which no suitable supervision appeared to have been exercised.

They were also of the opinion that after scientific examination, the boiler had been made of inferior iron and that it had latterly been worked in a very deplorable condition. They added that they strongly recommended that all steam boilers be placed under Government inspection.

Whilst the verdict pinpointed the later ownership and operation of the boiler, findings proved that the manufacture, repair and maintenance of the boiler prior to being sited at Bingley left many question marks which affected the final outcome.

Questions as to Hodgkinsons' previous work experience, low rate of pay, level of skill, the history of the boiler since its manufacture 12 years before and the siting of the mill so near a school were all discussed in depth as part of the inquest.

Neither was this an isolated incident. Figures for 1869 showed that there were upwards of 80 deaths per year as a direct result of boiler explosions!

## Tragic

When an accident of this nature happens within a community, recrimination is no solution. What happened in Bingley was that the townspeople assisted in the rescue, raised funds to support those affected, cared for the families of the bereaved and attempted to return to normality in the most difficult of situations.

In doing so it was appreciated that John Town had lost his son, daughter in law and grandchild as well as everything that he owned. Families had lost fathers, sons and daughters and would take generations to recover. Perhaps the most tragic aspect was that two young girls and seven boys were killed at the very start of their lives in an accident that was waiting to happen and could have been prevented.

# Milner Field – Walking in the Footsteps of Titus Salt Junior?

This Chapter seeks to add to knowledge of what Milner Field the home of Titus Salt Junior and family, and its grounds may originally have looked like when built 141 years ago.

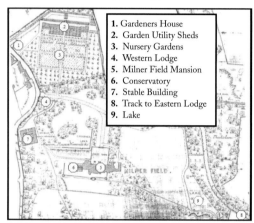

1. Gardeners House
2. Garden Utility Sheds
3. Nursery Gardens
4. Western Lodge
5. Milner Field Mansion
6. Conservatory
7. Stable Building
8. Track to Eastern Lodge
9. Lake

*Original map of Milner Field grounds*

## What might Titus have considered?

At a time when photography was in its infancy Titus Salt Junior would have had to rely on the vision of his architects and other contractors and their ability to convey design and building considerations to him. This would have been by means of maps, sketches, drawings and stained glass cartoons which gave more than a flavour of what was being suggested or recommended to him. In this chapter I will include images of some of these so that you the reader can try place yourself in his mindset. In doing so it is also my intention to "walk" you through the building and landscape.

## Purchasing the Land

Whilst there had been a smaller house on the site since 1400, primarily owned by the Milner then Oldfield, then Fell families, Sir Titus Salt bought the land for £21000 in 1869 from an Admiral Dunscombe and immediately demolished the house. Ownership then passed to Titus Salt Junior who proceeded to commission the building of a new house.

## Building the new Milner Field

On Monday 21st June 1869 the following advertisement appeared in the Bradford Observer.

As a result of the advertisement the main contractors commissioned were:

Shaftoe and Barry - York — General Contractors

Thomas Nichols- London — Stone and Wood Carving

Marsh, Jones and Cribb- Leeds — Furniture

Richardson, Slade and Co- London — Wrought Metalwork

Burke and Co- London — Chimney-pieces and metalwork

Robert Marnock - London — Gardens and Landscaping of the Park

Frederick Weekes – London — Paintings, Murals, Stained Glass Design

Saunders and Co- London — Making of Painted and Stained Glass

Thomas Harris – — Architect advised by Norman Shaw

*The Seven Ages cartoon of stained glass for Milner Field. Removed from the building at an unknown date*

85

*Park front*

*Milner Field,
rear entrance*

## Building Style

The style of the house was described in *Building News* 15th March 1873 as "*12th Century medieval, an assemblage of circular conical-capped towers, great chimney stacks and machicolations, all raised up on a terrace.*" The shell of the house was built over two years between 1871 and 1873 in the (then fashionable) neo-Gothic style. Opinion seemed to be divided between advocates of this style and critics such as John Ruskin who described the house as a Gothic monstrosity.

The material used in the construction was "*the grey local stone, the outer walls being lined with brick so as to form hollow walls and thereby prevent the possibility of dampness*" The roofs were covered with Whitland Abbey green slates bought and transported from Wales. *The Builder magazine* of March 15th 1873 reported that by that date "*internal decorations are now in progress.*"

## Equipment

What was clear from the very outset of the building programme was that considerable thought had been given to equipping the house with the most up to date equipment and facilities. These included: (see overleaf)

# Milner Field Floorplan of the Ground Floor

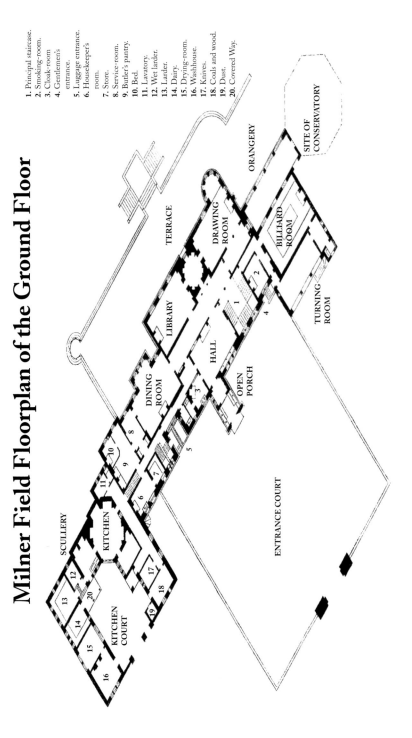

1. Principal staircase.
2. Smoking-room.
3. Cloak-room
4. Gentlemen's
   entrance.
5. Luggage entrance.
6. Housekeeper's
   room.
7. Store.
8. Service-room.
9. Butler's pantry.
10. Bed.
11. Lavatory.
12. Wet larder.
13. Larder.
14. Dairy.
15. Drying-room.
16. Washhouse.
17. Knives.
18. Coals and wood.
19. Dust.
20. Covered Way.

SCULLERY

KITCHEN

KITCHEN COURT

DINING ROOM

LIBRARY

TERRACE

HALL

DRAWING ROOM

OPEN PORCH

BILLIARD ROOM

ORANGERY

TURNING ROOM

SITE OF CONSERVATORY

ENTRANCE COURT

- An elaborate lighting system
- Own water piped from nearby natural springs
- An underground reservoir and canal to supply water to the Glasshouses in the Kitchen Garden
- Own filter beds for sewage disposal
- Telephonic systems connecting the house with the Saltaire Mill. An experiment between the Mill and Milner Field was carried out in September 1877 to enable this to happen. Later links were established with family in Halifax during 1879.
- Water cooled dairy's and storage rooms (the forerunner of refrigeration)
- Fire pumps and appliances for obtaining water at high pressure

**Travelling to the House from Saltaire**

After leaving Saltaire via what is now Victoria Road and originally crossing a stone bridge, Milner Field could be reached by a carriage drive along a private road westward below Shipley Glen, past Trench Farm and Fell Wood, before reaching South Lodge.

This lodge (also known as Bottom Lodge) was the start of an uphill climb to Milner Field using a long tree lined approach road through thick woodland. To the left of this road lay a small lake and fishpond with an island and rustic wooden bridge, a boathouse and several rowing boats. Eventually the road turned left to approach the entrance-way to the house.

Milner Field was built facing almost due north and south, the entrance being on the north (rear) side of the building through an arched gateway into a spacious enclosed courtyard. To catch the sun, the principal rooms of the house faced south and opened onto a wide terrace with steps leading down to the park.

**Entering Milner Field**

To enter the house from the rear courtyard visitors would pass through an outer porch and vestibule before arriving in the entrance hall. This space was dominated by a three manual organ built by Brindley and Fletcher of Sheffield and served as a music room as well as an entrance lobby.

*Building News* (1873) commenting about the inside of the building observed :"*The whole interior treatment has been kept in harmony with the style of architecture, all the fittings and much of the furniture have been made from special designs. Some of the rooms have handsome moulded open ceilings of oak, and woodwork in the principal apartments is either of walnut or chestnut, oak or cedarwood, whilst many of the windows are fitted with stained glass, the subjects being legendary, emblematical or symbolical."*

## Layout of the House

### East Wing

To the left of the entrance hall lay what was primarily the service wing of the house reached by a corridor which contained a house-keepers room, butler's pantry and a servery leading through to the dining room. An entrance from the courtyard onto this corridor was provided to enable visitors' luggage to be brought unobtrusively into the house.

At its far end the corridor led down some stairs to the kitchen, food preparation and storage areas and heating supply for the house. The octagonal shaped kitchen was designed to be a replica of the Glastonbury Abbey in medieval times.

### West Wing

To the right of the entrance hall was an arch which led through to the principal house staircase to the first floor, then past a smoking room to reach the billiard room. The billiard room also had a separate "Gentlemans Entrance" from the courtyard.

### First Floor Bedrooms

In total there were nine bedrooms, four facing north and looking out over the courtyard and croquet lawn, and five at the front of the building facing south and looking out over the parkland. Three toilets and bathrooms provided services to these rooms, some en-suite for occasions when there

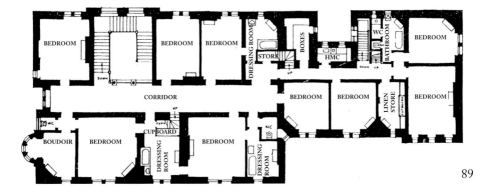

were visitors. At the far west end, with a front facing window and a side facing window next to the Conservatory was a bedroom with facilities, a boudoir and dressing room. This is the room where Royalty stayed on the two occasions that they visited Milner Field in 1882 and 1887.

## Front of the House

The principal rooms on the ground floor of the house were south facing in aspect and overlooked the terrace, which then had steps leading down to the parkland.

These rooms were reached from the entrance hall through arches on either side of the hall fireplace. The left hand arch led through to the dining room which had a corridor connecting it to the library. The right hand arch led through to the same corridor on which the drawing room was also sited. The library and drawing room were connected by an ante room which also led out of the front of the house on to the terrace. The corridor at its west end then became an orangery with mosaic tiled floor which led through to the conservatory.

## Conservatory

The Conservatory was a major feature attached at the west end front of the house and was eighty one feet long, forty feet wide and twenty six feet high and built with a dome shaped roof of iron and glass.

It had a chequered pattern mosaic tile floor and housed several life sized statues and an abundance of purpose built wicker garden furniture. Titus Salt Jr was an avid collector of exotics and in the conservatory he grew and

*The Conservatory*

displayed ornamental foliaged plants such as tree ferns, palms, yucca's, large auraucaria, dracaenas, aurelias and phormia. Lapagerias climbed to the roof on the south side and fuchias and clematis on the north side. On state occasions such as Royal visits the conservatory was lit up with Chinese lanterns.

## Grounds

Between 1869 and 1872 the Salt's employed Robert Marnock who was noted as, one of the greatest landscape designers of the 19th century. He was given the task of designing and planting the approach woodland to the house as well as the parkland and kitchen gardens.

As an advocate of the "gardenesque" style of natural planting and growth he planted yew, laurel and holly as principal woodland trees. Within this woodland lay the lake and fish pond.

As described already, the front of the house led onto a terrace and promenade which in turn gave access onto parkland. This was landscaped with lawns, plants and shrubs and had long distance views to Saltaire.

### Kitchen Gardens and Green houses

The Bradford Observer of 16th January 1873 carried an article on the Hothouses of Milner Field, the introduction of which stated:

*"Milner Field is a new garden – indeed it is yet in the process of being laid out by Mr Marnock. The principal houses are ranged side by side, lying due north to south; they are 34 feet long and 18 feet wide inside measure and are twelve in number.*

*All these houses open into a covered corridor, so that every house can be entered without exposing it to cold winds. The walks in the corridor are laid with cast iron plates three quarters of an inch thick and three feet wide, diamond pattern, supported on angle iron rails and cast iron pillars every six feet; this arrangement leaves the borders free for the roots of the vines & etc to run under the paths.........."*

The article then goes on to describe in great detail the arrangements for ventilation, heating and watering of the greenhouses, which like the equipment within the house were state of the art for the time. Amongst

*Rear of Milner Field with Conservatory on the right*

the greenhouses were those growing ferns, lapageria and roses and there were several forcing houses for plants for the Conservatory and gardens. There were also separate houses including hot and cool orchid houses, a vinery, a melon house, a fig house, a pineapple house and a mushroom cellar.

## Stables

The stables lay on the Primrose Lane side of the grounds near the Gilstead Lodge entrance to the estate. They are described as being extensive, and near to the house but sufficiently removed not to be intrusive. They contained automatic fodder hoists, sophisticated drainage systems and electric lights as well as storage for tack, hunting equipment and traps and landaus.

## Royal Visits to Saltaire

There were two well documented Royal visits where the royal guests stayed at Milner Field namely those of:

- The Prince and Princess of Wales when they opened the Bradford Technical College in June 1882
- Princess Beatrice and Prince Henry of Battenberg when they opened the Royal Jubilee Exhibition in May 1887

The Jubilee Exhibition ran from May 1887 until the end of October 1887.

## Death of Titus Salt Jr

Titus Salt Jnr died of heart disease on the afternoon of Saturday 19th November 1887 only nineteen days after the closing of the Jubilee Exhibition.

The heyday of Milner Field was in the period 1873 to 1887 when the Salts were renowned for their lavish entertaining.

After the death of Titus Salt Jr, Catherine his wife and George, one of his sons continued to live at the house until 1903. However in the intervening period and partly because of a trade slump Catherine was forced to sell the business to a syndicate of four Bradford business men, including James Roberts who within nine months became the Managing Director of Salts Mill.

Roberts moved into Milner Field in 1903. He and the next two residents of the house, Ernest Gates and A.R (Teddy) Hollins (a later Managing Director of Salts Co who died unexpectedly in 1929) all suffered a series of personal tragedies. This led many people to believe that the house was jinxed.

**What Became of Milner Field?**

The house was put up for sale in 1922 and 1930, but given the series of tragic events affecting all the owners and tenants, it is not surprising that the mansion subsequently failed to sell. Over the years nature reclaimed the grounds and the building fell into disrepair, was stripped of its contents and then of its roof, and before long the site began to be robbed of stone. During the Second World War it was reputedly used for grenade practice by the local Home Guard.

Whilst the exact date of demolition of the house is not known local legend suggests a date between 1950 and 1959.

Structures from the house such as part of the entrance arch and a small section of the mosaic floor to the Conservatory are still visible, as are the foundations to the greenhouses and cellars in the old kitchen gardens. Nowadays ownership of the land has passed to a holding company and discussion and decisions re the kitchen garden area becoming an area of specific scientific interest have taken place.

There is still much interest in the local area as to what Milner Field originally looked like and what became of the house and gardens. Perhaps this Chapter has gone some way towards satisfying curiosity about Milner Field, which may be gone, but is certainly not forgotten!

For readers seeking more information: *Milner Field - The Lost Country House of Titus Salt Jr* written by Richard Lee-Van den Daele and R David Beale and launched in 2011 is an invaluable rescource.

# The Glen – The Early Days

*Early amusements on Shipley Grlen*

This Chapter traces the early beginnings of tourism at what is now known as Shipley Glen. The following two Chapters will explore the development of a pleasure resort and rides on the Glen, and the establishment of the Japanese Gardens on Prod Lane.

## What's In A Name?

It would seem that the area including the Glen has at different times been known by different names and attributed to different townships. These include:

**Brackenhall Green/Brackenhall Crags/Brackenhall Glen** (up to about 1852) in Baildon

**Eldwick Glen** (up to about 1862) near Eldwick

**Shipley Glen** (first referred to in the Bradford Observer as such in 1863)

Cudworth (1875) in *Round and About Bradford* went as far as to say " *We come to Shipley Glen as it is wrongfully called, no part of the Glen being within a mile of any part of the township of Shipley..... The proper name is Bracken Hall Green and it is in the township of Baildon in the parish of Otley.*"

Varo (1980) in *Shipley Glen Ramble* observes that on the Ordnance Survey map of 1852, Shipley Glen was not noted. The first specific name given to this area of ground was Brackenhall Green.

Leake (2003) in *100 Years at Shipley Glen – The Story of the Glen Tramway* concurs when he states" *The name Shipley Glen does not exist on the map. The name was coined by the minister of the Bethel Chapel in nearby Shipley. The area is actually composed of Brackenhall Crag and Green, Trench Wood and Walker Wood.*"

The Leeds Mercury of March 5th 1881 confirms all the above when it notes "*The place called Shipley Glen is in the township of Baildon and not at any point connected to the township of Shipley. About forty years ago the place now called Shipley Glen had not the name Glen attached to it. It was then called Brackenhall Green and was not used as a place of public resort, nor was there any provision for the accommodation of visitors. After the Reverend Peter Scott, Baptist Minister of Shipley became acquainted with it and drew the publics' attention to its natural surroundings, it began to be called Shipley Glen, that being the only connection between the word Shipley and Glen.*"

**What Next?**

Several key historic events shaped the early development of the Glen

- The construction of the **railway line to Shipley** in 1846
- The opening of **Salts Mill** (1853) and phased building of Saltaire Village commencing 1854
- The opening of **Saltaire railway station** in 1856

Prior to these dates access to this beautiful tract of countryside had essentially only been open to those living in the immediate local area. However from 1846 newspaper records show that increasing numbers of people were using embryonic railway system and beginning to walk from Shipley Station and picnic in the area around the Glen. By 1852 individuals, church and Sunday School parties were regularly visiting the area from towns throughout West Yorkshire. As such the Glen according to newspaper reports of the time was gaining a reputation as:

"*A favourite retreat of pleasure seekers visited by thousands of persons*"

"*A beautiful place and great source of pleasure and healthy enjoyment*"

"*A place which cannot fail to please and gratify all lovers of nature*"

Conjecture suggests that because of the initial railway access via Shipley visitors would tell friends that they had "been to Shipley to visit the Glen"...hence Shipley Glen!

The Saltaire connection ensured that workers from Salts Mill used the Park and Glen in their few free hours as it was on their doorstep, and that the newly opened Saltaire station provided options for increasingly large numbers of visitors.

## However!

In 1854 there were a number of anonymous letters to the Editors of the Leeds Mercury and Bradford Observer newspapers debating the pro's and con's of conservation versus cultivation of Eldwick Glen and its future development. It was proposed by some that the area be purchased and developed as a Peoples' Park. A workers perspective is suggested in a letter signed "An Operative" sent in April 1854. The plea from the "Operative" seems to flow from an erudite and well educated pen!

*"I am a poor man. I live in a back street where ground is measured out by inches. Dark, ill looking dwellings, the hotbeds of disease are my only prospect. What wonder being so cooped up that I often pine for pure air, for the wide spreading moor and deep solitary glen.*

*I heartily concur in the design to secure Eldwick Glen for the public benefit. May the Glen be preserved and may the poor man be permitted to ramble undisturbed amongst its many beauties."*

In the event neither the concept of a Peoples' Park or cultivation of land for further quarrying or farming became a reality. The next phase of the development of the Glen in the 1850's however did involve two farm buildings on Brackenhall Green being converted to provide catering for the growing numbers of tourists.

### Temperance Hotels

A farm called Wood Head standing at the side of an old drovers road on Brackenhall Green was converted into the **Old Glen House and Hotel** by Charles Clegg in 1850. This small enterprise was believed to have been known as a Temperance Hotel which served afternoon teas to visitors. By 1875, the new owner

*Old Glen House and Hotel*

James Dewhurst and his family besides providing food had built boat swings and gave donkey rides in the garden.

A second old building on the Green, built originally as a cruck house was used by its owner William Cooper to sell refreshments under the name of the British Temperance Tea and Coffee House. The cruck house was demolished in 1885 and a wooden hut was built in the garden to provide catering. Part of this site is now the Brackenhall Countryside Centre.

*British Temperance Tea and Coffee House*

Large groups many connected with Church and Temperance Movements and Bands of Hope regularly visited the Glen in the period 1850 to 1870, to attend meetings, walk, picnic, or take tea. This explains in part the presence of Temperance Hotels on the Green.

An alternative for those who preferred alcohol was to extend their walk to the Fleece Inn at High Eldwick opened in a 1850 and run by Richard (Dick) Hudson (known today as **Dick Hudsons**). Many also used the pub as a stopping point for food before walking over the moors to Ilkley. This walk was particularly popular at Easter, Whitsun and Christmas holidays.

*Dick Hudsons*

## And Then...

Tourism in the 1870's and 1880's became more widely advertised and accessible due to expanding transport links and as a result people became more adventurous and sophisticated in their needs for relaxation and entertainment. Shipley Glen became a well visited and sought after venue on the tourist trail. Beautiful scenery alone was however insufficient and needed to be supplemented by other forms of entertainment to satisfy the requirements of a Victorian day out.

In 1887 the **Jubilee Exhibition** to celebrate Queen Victoria's Silver Jubilee was held in Saltaire from May until September. Besides showcasing British Industry and Commerce, one of the highlights of the Exhibition was the building of an entertainments area which provided refreshments and amusements. Within this area, a toboggan ride, camera obscura (more details in the next article), Japanese Village and a ride called the Ocean Wave Switchback were erected and proved very popular.

These would be used as the model for the Glen and consequently, each would be replicated over the next 13 years by local entrepreneurs and speculators as entertainment for the growing number of visitors to the Glen.

Within a year of the close of the Exhibition in 1887, the following had been installed on Brackenhall Green:

*Sam Wilson and his horse drawn tram*

**A horse drawn tram** which seated up to 20 people and which circled what was known as **Glen Pond** near to the Old Glen Hotel. Sam Wilson (who eventually expanded rides from and to the top of Shipley Glen), and a business partner, are rumoured to have bought six horse drawn open toast rack cars which had been used at the Saltaire Exhibition.

Two of these were said to have been used at Glen Pond and the others stored for later use on the Glen Tramway

A ride called the **Ocean Wave Switchback** which had been extremely popular at the Exhibition having averaged 3000 passengers per day between June and September 1887. This was erected at the side of the barn at Brackenhall Farm.

On 31 June 1888 the Leeds Mercury recorded:

*"The Switchback has been transferred from the Exhibition Grounds by some local speculators, to the top of Shipley Glen .Riding on the switchback is best described as sailing over large billows at a rapid rate."*

The Switchback was said to have been only the second made in the United Kingdom and had been made by Bainbridge and Bapty of Manchester. In typical Victorian language and detail a Leeds Mercury report of the time states:

*"The railway is built in the form of a series of ridges with the highest point 21 feet from the ground and falling to within 2 feet of it. The lines are about 150 yards long with boxed points at each end to enable the cars to run from one end to the other. Each car is built to accommodate 10 persons.*

*Having obtained its load of passengers the car is started down the first decline and the momentum thus gained carries it up the incline and over the ridges*

*and this operation is repeated until the end of the line is reached and the car stops within a few feet of its starting elevation. The occupants then dismount and take their seats in another car which awaits their arrival and are sent back to the starting point, the return line being exactly the same construction as the other. The cars are fitted with brakes and run of course on iron rails."*

Hopefully the ride was more exciting than the description!

## The Commercialisation of the Glen as a Tourist Resort

Having established the beginnings of entertainment on the Glen, Sam Wilson and others turned their thoughts to different forms of mechanised or white knuckle rides. The next Chapter will explore the development of the Aerial Flight, Toboggan, and Glen Tramway and the expansion of the Glen into a much more commercialised tourist resort.

# The Glen – Early Rides and New Experiences

Having previously identified the development up to 1888 of what came to be known as Shipley Glen, this Chapter looks at the establishing of the early entertainments, namely: The Camera Obscura, The Aerial Flight and The Toboggan Run. Whilst reference is made to the Glen Tramway (of which much has already been written) and the Vulcan House Pleasure Grounds, the text concentrates primarily on the less well known early rides.

## Developing Rides

The previous chapter described the relocating of the Ocean Wave Switchback from the 1887 Jubilee Exhibition at Saltaire, to the top of the Glen in June 1888. The ride was bought and installed by Mr J W Waddington. The ride became an instant hit and was renamed the Royal Yorkshire Switchback.

Taking their lead from the successful attractions at the Jubilee Exhibition, local entrepreneurs soon further captured the public's imagination in providing a variety of rides and experiences. By the end of the 1880's thousands of people were spending their Saturday and Sunday afternoons at the Glen.

## Camera Obscura

Possibly at the same time that the Switchback was re-sited on the Glen, the first of two giant camera obscura's was located close to Brackenhall Farm. In December 1887 an advertisement appeared in the Leeds Mercury announcing an auction of some of the effects of Jubilee Exhibition including: *"one camera obscura with lens, all complete and in excellent*

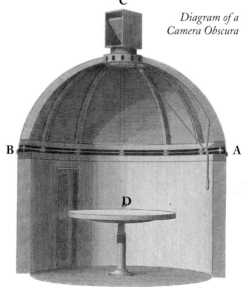

*Diagram of a Camera Obscura*

*condition, only been in use six months."* It is highly probable that by early 1888, this had been purchased as a novel attraction for the Glen.

For a small charge, a 360 degree view of the surrounding area could be viewed from inside the darkened hut which housed the obscura. A series of mirrors and prisms placed at the highest point of the roof (C) reflected light down through a lens below and onto a viewing table (D). The 360 degree view could be obtained by rotating the roof of the hut which ran on bearings, by handle (A and B (see diagram).

Other attractions were however less passive and not without their problems!

## The Aerial Flight

This is the attraction on the Glen about which least has to date been known. Through research I have managed to piece together some detail about the workings of the ride and its origins

### Blackpool Origins

In 1887 J W Stansfield patented and introduced the first Aerial Flight ride at the Royal Raikes Hall Gardens, Blackpool.

It was described in the Pall Mall Gazette as *"The world's first cable car ride, called the Aerial Flight which will become a rival to the switchback and toboggan. It is expected to eclipse both the older varieties of swift locomotion and as the cars glide through the air on wire ropes it affords the additional sensation of ballooning."* Stansfield started a company which he named the Stansfield Patent Aerial Flight Company.

### How Did it Work?

A description in the Liverpool Mercury in September 1888 explains the workings of the ride.....

*"Two wire ropes are stretched for some 150 yards or so, inclining from a station at a height of 60 feet to another station at about 20 feet. To these ropes cars are suspended by means of pulleys and when filled with eight passengers one car glides along the rope rapidly, its momentum being regulated only by the weight of the empty car on the second rope which is pulled up to the starting point in readiness for the next load of passengers."* Overleaf is an artists impression of Stansfield's patent.

### Unfortunately....

On September 11th 1888 one of the fastenings supporting the ropes became detached and seven people were injured, some seriously when the wooden car in which they were travelling fell thirty feet, hitting and demolishing a wall. The accident was widely reported in newspapers nationally.

*Stansfields Aerial Flight Patent*

### The Glen Aerial Flight

The Glen Aerial Flight was built in **1889, on the escarpment** at the top of the Glen by local men Badland and Halliday. However initially feelings ran high as an article in the Leeds Mercury on 18th March 1889 headed **Alleged Vandalism in Shipley Glen** reports:

*"No little commotion has been caused to the people who reside in the neighbourhood of Shipley and Saltaire by the appearance above the trees of a huge wooden skeleton which is to be utilised by speculators who hope to make money from thousands of holiday-makers who visit the Glen during the summer months. Something like a year ago the switchback railroad which had previously done duty at the Saltaire Exhibition was erected in a field on the plateau at the top of the Glen and this is certainly no improvement to the natural scenery, but the structure now being put up is something more offensive.*

*Instead of being fixed as much out of the general view as possible it holds the most prominent position overlooking the valley and is erected on what has always been considered common ground to which everybody has a right. It appears that fired by the success which has attended the switchback venture, a company called the Aerial Flight Company has been formed.*

*The Aerial Flight has two stations with an intervening line about 200 yards long. The platform of the first station is at a height of 45 feet from the ground the structure at the other end being not quite so high. Between the wooden starting station and terminus wire roping is fixed and on these ropes gondola cars are run conveying eight passengers from one end to another."*

## Comparison

From this description and comparing the photograph of the North East Tower of the Glen Aerial Flight to that of Stansfields Aerial Flight, it would appear likely that Badland and Haliday had knowledge of Stansfield's patent . Sam Halliday and his sons were blacksmiths and could well have adapted and built the Glen version of the Flight. They were later to be involved in building new cars for the Glen Tramway in the early 1900's.

*The Aerial Flight*

## Good Service

Stanley Varo (1984) in *Shipley Glen Ramble* describes the tranquil fashion in which *"passengers could be transported in a suspended cable car from Brackenhall Green, along the top of the escarpment to an area adjacent to the Old Glen House"*. The ride itself enjoyed great popularity during its years on the Glen and despite the initial objections gave good and safe service until it was closed in 1917 and finally dismantled in 1920.

## A Hard climb!

As the number of attractions on the Glen increased, so did the number of visitors. Many of them took the train to either Shipley or Saltaire then walked to the bottom of the Glen before climbing the steep bridleway up to Prod Lane and to the Glen. Having already established the Horse Drawn Tramway at the top of the Glen, local entrepreneur Sam Wilson and his partner Mr H Wilkinson spotted a business opportunity. **What if they were to build a cable tramway beside the bridleway to relieve visitors of the tiring climb?** Consequently, they started negotiating land purchase firstly with Sam Roberts the owner of Salts Mill and then with local landowner Colonel Maude.

## Shipley Glen Tramway

The Tramway was opened on 18th May 1895 but the 350 metre long track was shorter than originally envisaged due to the unsuccessful negotiations with the owner of Salts Mill. Despite this initial setback the Tramway proved to be an immediate and lasting success. On Easter Monday 1910 it is rumoured that it carried a record 17,000 visitors out of the estimated 100,000 who visited the Glen that day! The Yorkshire Film Archives online have an eight minute film of the event.

The full history of the Tramway is well detailed in Leak (2003) *100 Years at Shipley Glen – The Story of the Glen Tramway*. After recent repairs I understand that the Tramway is again running and seeking volunteers to assist and ensure its future.

## Pleased Customers!

Two articles from West Yorkshire newspapers written in 1895 perhaps best capture the popularity that the Glen was gaining with its growing number of visitors:

Huddersfield Chronicle 29th June 1895 - Crosland Moor Wesleyan Chapel Choir visit to Shipley Glen. "*Passing through Saltaire we proceeded up the beautiful Glen, some walking and some riding up the new Glen Tramway and all admiring the beautiful scenery which abounds*" Tea had been arranged for us at the **Old Glen House** at about 4.30 and the party sat down to an excellent tea.

*Later, we proceeded higher up the Glen, the younger and more frolicsome members were quickly enjoying the switchback railway and the aerial flight whilst the older and more staid members rambled about.*"

Bank Holiday Leeds Mercury 6th August 1895. "*The new Tramway up Glen Wood was unable to carry all the passengers who sought its aid to mount the hill. On the plateau of the Glen itself the switchback and aerial flight were popular.*"

## The Toboggan Run

The Baildon Building Plan Registers show that In February 1896, Sam Wilson put in an application to to build a toboggan ride. His intention was to replicate the toboggan slide which had been a success at the Jubilee Exhibition, but on a much larger and more spectacular scale.

In doing so he built in 1898 what was called "*The Largest, Wildest and Steepest Toboggan Ride Ever Erected on Earth!*" consisting of wooden tracks which descended at an estimated 1 in 4 gradient from the rocky escarpment at the top of the Glen to the valley floor at the bottom. Riders seated in small wooden toboggans hurtled down the run which ended in a slight uphill gradient that with the assistance of car brakes finally slowed the cars down.

The passengers then returned to the top of the Glen by a cable tram car which also carried the returning car in front , both being hauled back up to the top by steel hawser driven by a gas engine.

*Sam Wilson and his Toboggan Run*

## Major Accident

On Whit Monday 1900 one of the returning cars caught the cable pulling it, causing it to snap. The car carrying twelve people ran back down the slope at speed and crashed at the bottom. Eleven people were hurt, six seriously. The injured were treated at Sir Titus Salt Hospital, Saltaire.

A report in the Essex County Observer 9th June 1900 stated:*"An accident which resulted in serious injury to several holidaymakers at Shipley Glen a favourite resort for Bradford and Leeds people occured on Monday night.*

*One of the attractions of the glen is the toboggan slide which was fixed some years ago down the steep side of the glen and has been described as the biggest toboggan slide in existence. The wire rope used to haul the cars up the slide broke and a dozen people were precipitated with great force against the bottom of the toboggan ride."*

*Toboggan Run after accident*

Sam Wilson immediately closed the run and within twelve months it had been dismantled.

## Finally - The Development of Prod Lane

As the Glen developed and flourished as a tourist attraction, Prod Lane, which visitors would pass on their way to the Glen, also benefited and developed in tandem.

One location, Vulcan House, built in 1879 seized the chance to open a tearoom which was soon frequented by thousands of visitors. Application was received from J W Perry as early as November 1879 by Baildon Building Planning Committee, seeking permission to build a "refreshment room". Eventually the tearooms began to introduce rides and amusements of their own, but on a smaller scale. This area would later become known as the Shipley Glen Pleasure Grounds.

*Vulcan House Amusements*

A ride called the Aerial Glide (not to be confused with the Aerial Flight) was also built and a Zoo known initially as Marsden's Menagerie was instituted.

Another highly popular attraction, the Japanese Gardens also opened on Prod Lane and is covered on page 109.

## 2011

In 2011, of all the rides, only the Glen Tramway still exists, the other attractions having been demolished as other forms of entertainment and the advent of the car drew visitors to more exotic and more distant locations. Local land development, safety considerations and economics also had an effect on commercial aspects of the area around the Glen.

Today the Glen has essentially returned to its original utilisation as a destination for new generations of families and walkers who enjoy a walk and a picnic in the fresh air. Whatever its uses the Glen still represents a much loved and visited asset in the local area.

# The Glen - The Development of the Japanese Gardens

One of the much loved amusements at the Glen did not owe its origins to the need for thrills or excitement. Instead it offered a more tranquil and sedate pace of passage in quiet and landscaped surroundings. This experience was known as the Japanese Gardens and was the brainchild of Thomas (Tom) Hartley of Bowling, Bradford.

Prior to being proprietor of the Japanese Gardens, he is identified in the 1871 Census as a General Dealer living and working in Bowling in Bradford and in 1881 as an Ironmonger still living in Bowling.

## Ivy House – Prod Lane

In 1886 Tom went to live at Ivy House, Prod Lane, Baildon with his wife and family. According to rumour and local knowledge, Hartley was a businessman friend of Titus Salt's son, Titus Junior. When Hartley's wife became ill, Salt seemingly advised him to move to Shipley Glen for the quality of the air.

It seems that at the time, Japanese Gardens were very fashionable and were being built in the grounds of large houses around the country. Hannah Hartley, now an invalid who was confined to bed for long periods of time, longed to see them but was too ill to travel. The Jubilee Exhibition in Saltaire had in 1887 contained a Japanese Village as an entertainment attraction. This may have been the stimulus for Tom to build his own version for his wife so that she could look from her bedroom window and see them below.

## Not Japanese but .........

An article entitled *The State of Horticulture in Britain, With an Eye to Japanese Gardening in the 1890's* pointed out that "*The scale-model approach dominated most early attempts at Japonaiserie in the garden. The 'Japanese' garden at Ivy House, Shipley Glen, laid out in the 1880s by a Yorkshireman named Thomas Hartley, contained a miniature lake and islands, one carrying two pagoda arches but on the other stood a miniature castle with no Japanese connotations.*"

## The Castle and Arches

Thomas built a pond with islands in the middle, on which he constructed a small folly in the shape of a ruined castle and surrounded by rustic arches. The castle and arches were built from clinker, the cinders forming one of the first concrete structures built in the area. These structures were covered with white lime. In an attempt to give them a rough and rustic appearance he used the waste dross reputedly taken from the fireboxes of the steam trains which travelled from Bradford to Saltaire. Locals observed Mr Hartley wheeling the material by the barrow-load through the woods and up the hill.

## The Pond

The Pond was set in the midst of beautifully landscaped flower beds, For a small charge a boatman would stand upright and propel passengers in a flat bottomed boat (originally called the Saucy Sue) around a number of circuits Near the pond and still in line with his wife's bedroom window Hartley built a smaller pond with a fountain, surrounded by archways over the paths and below the second pond was a water-lily pool.

The water for the ponds was provide by a stream running down Hope Hill from the top of Baildon Moor, which he diverted and rechanneled so that the water was flowing continuously.

Further back from the ponds he built two glass houses, one with a stream running through and a small waterfall with an enormous hydrangea and other plants. The other housed an aviary containing exotic birds, love birds and doves. Between the two was a small amusement arcade with penny slot machines.

Hartley filled the garden with trees including lilac, orange blossom and laburnum complimented by roses and many other beautiful flowers. At the back of Ivy House he built a tea room which had a hut, with long wooden tables and wooden benches as seats.

## Advertising and Postcards

Tom obviously had an eye for marketing the various aspects of his gardens as the advertisement opposite from 1904 shows.

In it you can see him working in the garden below the window from which his wife would have viewed the garden pond. Also advertised are swings (these were boat swings), see-saws and a grotto. The enterprise also offered the opportunity for visitors to have their photograph professionally taken using the gardens as a backdrop. Failing this, Tom also sold postcards of the gardens and pond.

## . . HARTLEYS' . .

 # JAPANESE GARDENS,

## SHIPLEY GLEN.

Visitors to the Glen should on no account fail to visit these **Novel** and **Interesting Gardens**. Ample provision for their amusement and enjoyment is provided, consisting of

## SWINGS, SEE-SAWS, GROTTO, Etc.

## Picturesque Photographic Studio with Rustic Background.

**Where you may have a Photograph taken which will do both justice to yourself and to the photographer.**

### Miniature Circular Lake

On which is a small boat that has proved a great favourite with both young and old.

### Cut Flowers & Bouquets.

Do not fail to make a call and we venture to say that you will not regret it.

**Closed entirely on Sundays.**

111

Cut flowers and bouquets from the garden were also sold to visitors. The 1901 Census describes Tom as working from home, on his own account as a Market Gardener.

The advert also shows that the gardens were "*closed entirely on Sundays.*" This was because the Hartleys were staunch Methodists.

## Weight and Fortunes

Near to the entrance to the Japanese Gardens there was a set of old fashioned weighing scales where visitors could pay a small amount to be weighed. Alongside sat a fortune teller who had a budgerigar which would pick a playing card to be used by fortune teller to predict your future.

## Changes In Ownership

Unfortunately Hannah Hartley died and later when Tom remarried he built a bungalow for himself and his new wife and a bungalow for his son at the back of the gardens circa 1901.

The Japanese Gardens as an entity were sold to Tom Clark who lived at Ivy House until 1918 when he decided to divide the gardens into two. In one part he built a bungalow for himself, which was in line with the two that Tom Hartley had built. He retained the boat and swings for himself and opened a baker's and confectioners shop at the side of the bungalow.

He sold Ivy House, the other half of the garden and the tea rooms to Harry Clark who then ran the tearooms until 1924.

From that date ownership then passed to the Theakston brothers, John and on his early death, George. His granddaughter Margaret Ellis in recounting family memories to custodians of the Shipley Glen Tramway and to Roger Clarke, the Saltaire historian has highlighted:

- The early Sunday mornings (by now introduced) when helpers and family would prepare vast amounts of bread and buns for visitors and serve these at the counter in the tearoom.

- Members of the family helping by punting the Saucy Sally boat around the pond using a long pole and rescuing and drying those who regularly fell in the water!

- The opportunity for young family members to swim in the pond and play hide and seek round the castle and archways when all the visitors had left.

*Thomas Hartley at Ivy House laying out the original Japanese Gardens*

*Original layout of the
Pond, Castle and Arches*

*Tom Hartley Jr and
the Rustic Arches*

- The annual visits to the gardens and pond by the Blind Institute in Bradford and of many Sunday Schools. The venue was also frequented by cycling clubs from throughout Yorkshire who would arrive and spend their day in the gardens and on the moors, having pots of tea at the start and end of their day.

- V. E Day in 1945 when Shipley Glen was inundated with celebrating visitors and upwards of five hundred people were queuing in the tearoom at one time.

**Beginning of the End**

It appears that after the Second World War it became harder to make a go of the enterprise although throughout the 1950's The Glen was still a popular destination.

Over time the once glorious gardens began to deteriorate as the advent of the car meant that fewer visitors came to the area. The original house and gardens were sold in 1975 and the land used for housing development.

Tom Hartley the original and proud creator of the Japanese Gardens died at the age of 99 in 1944. He like the many visitors over the years would have been saddened by the eventual demise of this much loved local attraction.

Perhaps the final words are best left to Margaret Ellis and her family memories of the Japanese Gardens: "*Now all that is left of the late Victorian/ early Edwardian pleasure gardens are older folks' memories of halcyon summer days when they were young and their recollections of the warmth and happiness of a lost age.*"

# SECTION
# FOUR

The 1900's

# Lily Cove – Parachute Tragedy at Haworth Gala

*Lily Cove*

Lily Cove was a happy go lucky twenty one year old from East London who made a name for herself as a fearless and daredevil parachutist. She travelled the country with Captain Frederick Bidmead a stunt balloonist who was her manager, performing at fetes and gala's where she jumped from a balloon and parachuted to the ground. Bidmead is reputed to have made 83 parachute descents in his career, and had already appeared at Keighley fund raising events for the local hospital in 1898 and 1900.

## Haworth Gala

By 1906 Lily had made twenty one ascents by balloon and six descents by parachute without accident (Recks, 1983) *Who's Who of Ballooning*) In that year she was asked by Haworth and Oxenhope United Friendly Societies and Tradesmen's Association to perform as the main feature at the local Gala, to raise money for the Haworth and Oxenhope District

Nurses Association. She and Bidmead arrived in Haworth the day before the planned event and stayed at the White Lion Hotel.

**First Attempt**
The balloon ascent and parachute jump were fixed for the Gala Day on Saturday 9th June 1906 and the balloon was filled with gas from the local gas works. However, after six or seven attempts at launching over a period of ninety minutes the balloon failed to rise into the air. This was thought to be due to the heavy atmosphere and poor "lifting" qualities of the local gas.

In order not to disappoint the large crowd estimated at 6,000, Bidmead and Lily agreed to attempt the balloon flight and parachute jump early the following week. This event took place from West Lane Football Field on Monday 11th June 1906 which was a warm summers evening, perfect for the attempt.

The sequence of events of that evening are recorded by Campbell (2001) in *The Strange World of the Brontes*. For the purposes of this chapter I have supplemented some of this information with local, national and international newspaper reports and will summarise events as they happened.

**Second Attempt**
The balloon was successfully inflated, there was little breeze, the light was good and all the conditions were favourable for a successful performance in front of seven thousand spectators. Prior to the flight Lily and Bidmead checked the condition of the balloon. Lily then stepped on to the launch platform before taking her seat and fastened herself to a trapeze hanging underneath the balloon.

*Lily on the trapeze with parachute attached to the side of the balloon*

At precisely 7.40pm the balloon was released and rose steadily into the air with Lily waving to the crowd with a white handkerchief, whilst they watched the balloon drift towards Stanbury.

The plan was that once she reached sufficient altitude, Lily would detach herself from the trapeze and in doing so a line attached to the balloon would release and open her parachute. She would then hopefully float safely to earth.

## The Accident
In the event, the balloon ascended to 700 feet and at about 7.45pm, Lily jumped. Her parachute opened as planned and she descended to one hundred feet. It was at this stage that Robert Rushworth of Stanbury who was monitoring her progress, observed her shrugging her shoulders out of the safety harness for no apparent reason, as she neared Ponden reservoir. In doing so she detached herself from her parachute and plummeted to the ground head first, landing in a field near the reservoir.

Cowling Heaton who ran the nearby Scar Top Refreshment Rooms was first on the scene followed by Bidmead and a local mill owner C E Merrall who had been tracking the balloon in a pony and trap. Although Lily was breathing slightly she died within moments of their arrival. Her body was placed in the back of the pony and trap and taken back to Haworth where it was laid out in her room at the White Lion Hotel until a coffin could be made for her.

## The Inquest
At approximately 9pm that evening, a local doctor Robert Thompson examined Lily's body and found fractures of both legs and her right thigh and severe bleeding caused by a skull fracture. At the subsequent inquest at Haworth, a number of reasons for her death were speculated on including the fact that she had taken her own life. No evidence was presented that affirmed a reason for this.

Captain Bidmead gave the inquiry his opinion that Lily had deliberately separated herself from the parachute because she was drifting towards Ponden reservoir and as a non-swimmer had an absolute fear of water. Consequently she decided to escape the possibility of drowning by loosening herself from her parachute, whilst also possibly misjudging that she was nearer the ground than she was.

Cowling Heaton who had witnessed the accident at close quarters, said that had Lily remained in her parachute (which landed partially open twenty yards from her body), she would have lived. Campbell (2001) observes *"Whatever the truth of the matter, it died with Lily."*

The inquest jury found a verdict of "Death by Misadventure" and decided to recommend to the Home Secretary that such exhibitions should be made illegal.

## The Funeral

On 14th June 1906 after a short service attended by Lily's father Thomas Cove and friends, the funeral cortege made its way to the cemetery from the Old White Lion. The whole village turned out to mourn her and members of the Haworth Gala Committee carried her coffin. The District Nurses Association took up a collection which paid for the granite gravestone which bore the inscription below.

On the day of Lily's funeral Parliament was already preparing a Dangerous Performance Bill supported by Mr Gladstone the Home Secretary.

## The Dangerous Performance Bill

Lily was the fourth woman to die in this manner since the first lady balloonist took to the air in Paris in 1784. In the UK the notable fatalities were:

1895 - Adelaide Bassett died at Peterborough when she desscended through telegraph lines that destroyed her parachute and caused her to fall sixty feet to her death.

1902  - Edith Brookes died at Hillsborough Park, Sheffield when her parachute failed to open on descent.

*Hansard* (Volume 158) 14th June 1906 records the following exchange between Arthur Fell, MP for Great Yarmouth and Herbert Gladstone (Leeds West) the Home Secretary, in the House of Commons:

Fell: "*I beg to ask the Secretary of State for the Home Department whether his attention has been called to the death of Miss Cove when descending from a balloon in a parachute on June 11th; and whether he proposes to take any steps to prohibit such exhibitions in the future.*"

Gladstone: "*My attention has been called to this shocking case. I have prepared, and hope to introduce shortly, a Bill extending the Dangerous Performances Acts to all women whatever their age may be.*"

## International Reports

The tragedy was also reported internationally as was captured by the following headline and comment in the New York Times of July 1 1906:

### Dangerous Turns by Women May Be Stopped in England

"*A recent announcement was made by Mr Herbert Gladstone the English Home Secretary that the Government proposed to initiate legislation with a view to stopping dangerous performances by women. The tragic death of Miss Cove by the failure of her parachute has brought the question forward in the most urgent manner.*"

Two months after the Haworth Gala, the Hawera and Normanby Star (27 August 1906)  in New Zealand carried the story *Dashed to Death – Parachute Descent Ends in Disaster* giving a full account of what had happened to Lily at Haworth.

So, Haworth is not just a stop on the tourist trail, a nice place to visit at weekends, or solely the home of the Bronte family. As this chapter has hopefully shown it has other history which in this case had an effect on the local, the national and the international scene, from what at first might appear to be a local event only.

# The Hidden Valley - Harden, Wilsden and Cullingworth's Best Kept Secret?

*Goit Stock Waterfall*

**This chapter explores the history of an area which is still little known to many people living in the Aire Valley.**

## Introduction

Over the last 200 years the Hidden Valley has been the site of a cotton mill, a beauty spot from the mid 1800's and a much visited tourist attraction in the 1920's. The valley extends from Hallas Bridge, and past Goit Stock Waterfall at one end, down to what was the site of Goit Stock Cotton Mill (now a Residential Park Homes Estate) at the other. It can be accessed from either end by following Harden Beck through the woods.

The area was primarily owned by the Ferrand family as part of the St Ives Estate until they sold it in 1919.

## Goit Stock Waterfall

Access to this renowned beauty spot was restricted during the 18th and early 19th Century's.

Speight (1898) *Chronicles of Old Bingley* states:

"*The Goit Stock waterfall is in Mr Ferrands private grounds. It is a beautiful retired spot, the white crested water falling over a hard rocky cliff about twenty feet high, into a deep pool below, the whole embosomed in a luxuriant and lofty screen of trees, making a perfect fairy dell, which is lit up by the slanting sunbeams with charming effect.*"

This sentiment and flowery style of writing may seem very old-fashioned to the modern reader, however the beauty of the waterfall is undisputed and nowadays still continues to delight visitors.

## The Airedale Poet

In earlier times another writer with poetic ambitions waxed lyrical about Goit Stock. In 1820 John Nicholson, later to be known as the Airedale Poet moved to Harden Beck where he gained the practical friendship of the Horsfall family at Goit Stock Mill, who helped to support him. His wife also helped his writing ambitions by working at a local worsted mill during the time he was composing "*Airedale*" the poetic work for which he is perhaps most famous. Horsfall –Turner (1897) in *Ancient Bingley* notes "*He (Nicholson) composed when wandering on moonlight nights along the beck-side, especially near Goit Stock Waterfall.*"

Seemingly Nicholson found the peace and tranquillity of the time of day and of the walk to be an aid to his writing and meditation. In a poem about the area he makes reference to the peaceful surroundings and the waterfall (cataract) when he observes:

"*Here may the contemplative mind*

*Trace Nature and her beauties o'er*

*And meditation rest reclin'd*

*Lull'd by the neighbouring cataract's roar*"

Nicholson on completing *Airedale* moved from Harden and worked as a woolsorter for three years at Hewenden Mill. He spent time after this roaming the country including living in London, promoting and selling his poetry. He eventually returned to Yorkshire and worked for Titus Salt in Bradford. He died of exposure in 1843 after falling in the River Aire while crossing by the stepping stones at was later to be Saltaire .

## Goit Stock Cotton Mill - Harden

Records show that in the late 18th Century, Benjamin Ferrand the owner of the St Ives Estate set Timothy Horsfall up in business by building a mill for him in the Goit Stock Valley. Horsfall was spinning cotton there at least in 1802 (Dodd (1930) *Bingley*) and lived with his wife Sarah and eleven children in a house adjoining the mill.

The mill was sited next to Harden Beck which fed a lake about 6 feet deep and which covered several acres behind the house. From here a mill-race ran through a wide bore pipe to a water wheel housed in a deep pit. The force of the water drove the wheel which measured 36 feet in diameter and was 9 feet wide and provided the motive power for the spinning frames. Kent (1993 - *What's That Chimney up There?*) observes the above and also that "*Steam came early to the valley and the cheaper but less reliable water power gave way to the steam engine making Goit Stock Mill one of the first in the area to use this innovation.*"

*Goit Stock Mill lake*

## Innovation

The mill was originally built as a three storey building and Kent (1993) records that each floor had 34 windows which made maximum use of the daylight. A newspaper account by The Liverpool Mercury on 28th November 1823 reported "*A Cotton Mill at Goit Stock, Harden has been raised a storey by the application of hydraulic presses*". *This was achieved by raising the roof in stages to accommodate a further floor.*" It seems that the mill and mill owners were known both locally and nationally for their innovative approaches to power and building!

## The Demise of the Mill as a Mill

Peter Smith in the *Yorkshire Journal* (Issue 46-Autumn 2004) *Deep in the Woods* observes that by the mid 1860's, cotton and cotton spinning had fallen out of favour in the local area. As a result Timothy Horsfall had already transferred his interests from cotton to wool and successfully set up a new business in Bradford.

As early as 1848 the Goit Stock Mill machinery, water wheel, steam engine and boilers had been advertised for auction in the Bradford Observer and Leeds Mercury. In February 1855 the water wheel, a Cornish boiler and power looms plus carts and horses were again advertised for auction in the Bradford Observer.

## Poultry Breeding in the Mill

The mill lay empty until 1865 when Henry Beldon a nationally renowned poultry breeder and exhibitor rented the building. Beldon fitted out part of the mill interior with pens and enclosures for the different varieties of chickens, hens and cockerels that he bred. He became one of the most successful exhibition and agricultural show breeders in the United Kingdom. Wright (1873) in *The Illustrated Book of Poultry* was impressed by the scale of Beldon's operation and commented:

"*As an example of quite different management of poultry we refer to the establishment of Mr Henry Beldon of Goitstock, Bingley, Yorkshire.*

"*Undoubtedly he has the largest poultry house in England in the shape of an old disused mill, which showed no sign whatever outside of the novel use to which it was devoted. The immense building measured about one hundred and twenty feet by thirty feet in plan and consisted of four floors, all of which were occupied by fowls. Two floors were devoted entirely to rows of pens about ten feet square down each side of the building, each pen having a window and a*

125

*wide passage being left down the middle". The other floors were left more open but accommodated many birds."*

After fifteen years of successful occupation of the building Beldon vacated the mill in 1880.

*Goit Stock Hall and Dam in 1897*

Access to the Ferrand land up to it being sold in 1919 was restricted to those who applied to the estate for a permit to walk on the land. Consequently the old mill appears to have been neglected and used for storage up until its conversion and opening in 1920 as a Dance Hall and Restaurant as part of the Happy Valley Resort.

## Happy Valley Pleasure Resort

In 1920 a tourist attraction was opened up in the grounds of the old mill site. Called Happy Valley Pleasure Resort – Goit Stock, the main attraction was the adaptation of the old mill to house a purpose built dance hall on one floor and a large 1000+ seat tearoom/cafe serving refreshment during the day, on another floor. On the ground floor there was an alfresco and more informal tea-pavilion for light refreshments which served visitors on terraces overlooking a lawn where outdoor dancing took place.

An advertising brochure of the time claimed:

*"Many factors combine to make this Popular Pleasure Resort, which is situated in the beautiful Harden Valley, a centre of great attraction for Holiday parties.*

Delightful walks and richly wooded slopes abound in all directions, whilst the majestic waterfalls never fail to captivate the eye in regions of enchanting beauty. Spacious grounds are provided for the children, who can partake in unlimited forms of games and amusements.

The well appointed **Ballroom** meets the demands of those interested in dancing and lovers of this popular pastime are assured of every consideration on their behalf.

There is an up-to-date **cafe** with accommodation for over 1000 at one sitting. Everything served is of the best quality at reasonable prices".

Goit Stock Mill Tearoom/Cafe

Goit Stock Mill Ballroom

*Goit Stock Fun Park*

## Attractions in the Grounds

The grounds provided amusements which catered for all family age groups.

These included a Childrens Corner and paddling pool, swings and a small toboggan run. The old mill lake was turned into a boating lake, whilst other parts of the grounds offered a bowling green and miniature golf course to visitors. An aviary and monkey house were built on site and there was an ornate bandstand used by the Wlisden Brass Band to play concerts during the day.

For those who wanted to experience the woods and grounds there were kiosks selling snacks and for those wanting to sleep under canvas, a purpose built Holiday Camp was available. Fishing in the lake and Harden Beck were also provided for those interested in "the great outdoors."

## Saturdays and Seasonal Events

Costume Concert Parties, popular at the time, gave performances in the grounds every Saturday and on Bank Holidays during the season. Holiday periods covered Easter Monday and Tuesday, Whit Monday and Tuesday and the August Bank Holiday. Other annual events included a May Carnival, July Music Festival, August Athletic Meeting and Carnival and a September Grand Firework Display.

What were advertised as first class bands performed every Saturday and holiday during the season, brochures stating: *"All the up-to-date music is played by the Goit Stock Orchestra"* Dances were held either in the ballroom or weather permitting, on the lawns.

## Transport and Admission

Happy Valley could be reached by train to Cullingworth or Bingley stations. Tram services via Wilsden or Bingley were also available, the last stage of the journey being made by motorised charabanc. Admission to the pleasure-grounds was 6d for adults and 3d for children.

## The Happy Valley Fire Disaster 1927

The resort became an increasingly popular attraction as the 1920's progressed. So much so, that an estimated 20,000 people visited the site on Easter Monday 17th April 1927. Unfortunately, disaster struck Happy Valley on that day.

A report in the Keighley News on Saturday 23rd April 1927 carried the headline **Destructive Fire at Goit Stock - £10000 Damage**. At about 11.55 a guest who was staying with the Manager, Mr J Dewhirst at his house in the grounds noticed flames coming from the tearoom.

He immediately rang the Bingley Fire Brigade.

The flames spread so rapidly that within half an hour only the four bare walls of the former mill building were left standing. By the time the Fire Brigade arrived the floors and the roof had already caved in and there was little hope of saving the building They also had difficulty in getting an adequate supply of water to douse the flames. Despite these difficulties, the Fire Brigade subdued the flames by 3 am. The heat of the blaze was so intense that it melted the glass in the windows of the building.

The cause of the fire had not been established but it was noted that the ballroom had been "*made festive with bunting and streamers for a Carnival held during the day on Easter Monday.*" It was thought that perhaps a lighted cigarette had been thrown away and caused decorations to smoulder and eventually burst into flame.

Amongst items lost in the blaze were the instruments of the resident Dance Band and also the instruments of the Wilsden Brass Band who had been playing in the grounds all day for the enjoyment of the crowds. Mr J White , Conductor of the Wilsden Brass Band estimated that the instruments and music destroyed worth worth £200.

## The Demise of Happy Valley Pleasure Grounds

Despite attempts at refurbishment after the fire, things were never the same again for the enterprise. One of the last attempts at reviving interest was a ten round boxing match held at Goit Stock between Percy Vere (note the play on words!) of Crossflatts and Billy Shaw of Leeds (who won) in May 1932.

In October 1932 Happy Valley and its effects came under the auctioneers hammer. Amongst items sold were: the rebuilt ballroom, the boxing ring, the monkey house, monkeys, ponies donkeys and love-birds. The estate including the pleasure ground was sold for £2700.

## The Hidden Valley 1932 to 2011

Since the 1930's the site has passed through several hands and ideas for use of the land for forestry, building development and even a country gentleman's club have been mooted. Work by previous owners including George Reynolds, and later David and Adriane Sharples, who bought the site in 1979, has preserved the site as a desirable area for residential Park Homes, touring and static caravans.

Current owners of Harden and Bingley Park Homes Estate, Paul Davis and Julie Dunham have further developed the site which continues to provide an attractive environment for visitors and permanent residents alike.

Some of the original mill-workers cottages still exist alongside a meadow in which there is a single ancient chimney which has a slight lean to it. This is all that remains of the original Goit Stock Mill. As the title of a brief history of the area in 1993, author Alana Kent posed the question "*What's that Chimney up There?*" My answer is that it is a beacon that calls those in the know to the Hidden Valley and marks a Happy Valley where adults and children alike have enjoyed and continue to enjoy some of the best scenery that our local area has to offer.

# The Hindenberg over the Aire Valley – Mercy Errand or Spying Flight?

75 years ago on May 23rd 1936 the airship Hindenberg altered her course from her regular flight route and made the first of what were to be three flights that year over the **Aire Valley**. Other flights were made on June 30th and October 12th 1936.

## Questions in Parliament

The Hindenberg flight paths on these occasions were either from Frankfurt and then across Northern England to Lakehurst (New York) USA or the reverse on the return journey. The Hindenberg was essentially banned by the British and French Governments from flying across either country unless forced to do so by bad weather. The weather was reported to be fine on all these dates. Questions were asked in Parliament on 11th June and 8th July as to the legitimacy of these flights over what were considered to be "prohibited" areas in the North of England.

Sitings were also made at Blackpool, Nelson, Barrow in Furness, Morecambe, Lancaster, Barnoldswick, Earby, Gargrave, Crosshills, Kildwick, Skipton, Keighley, East Morton, Riddlesden, Harden, Bingley, Cottingley, Saltaire, Shipley, Bradford, Pudsey, Rawdon and Leeds, Thorne, Goole, Cromer and Grimsby.

## Flight over Keighley

Press records of the time show the dropping of a crucifix and a bunch of carnations from the airship over Keighley at 7.55pm on 23 May by a priest commemorating the death of his brother, a prisoner of war who in 1919 had died of influenza at Morton Banks Fever Hospital

The Yorkshire Observer reported:

*"A parcel floated down. Two boys ran to pick it up. They found a spray of fresh carnations, a tiny silver cross and a letter signed on Hindenberg notepaper which stated."*

*" To the finder of this letter, please deposit these flowers and the cross on the grave of my dear brother Lieutenant Franz Schulte 1st Garde Regiment Zu Foss, prisoner of war in Skipton, in Keighley near Leeds. Many thanks for your kindness John P Schulte, the first flying priest.*

*Please accept the stamps and picture (of the Hindenberg) as a small souvenir from me.*

*God bless you."*

My research has shown that the two boys were Alfred Butler and Jack Gerrard of Keighley, two Boy Scouts who found the parcel in the rear yard of a shop in High Street while on their way to an evening meeting. They were taken by a photographer from the Yorkshire Observer to the cemetery at Morton where the flowers and cross were placed on a memorial to forty German officers. After this act had been carried out the Yorkshire Observer Editor sent a radiogram to Herr Schulte on board the Hindenberg notifying him " *Flowers have been laid on Franz Schulte's grave.*"

(In 1959 the bodies of the Germans buried at Morton Cemetery were reinterred at the German Cannock Chase Cemetery, Staffs, where Franz Shulte's grave can be found at the bottom of the right hand slope)

## Flight over Bingley

After leaving Keighley the airship appeared over Bingley at about 8.04 pm *"flying at great speed and at a low altitude, the name Hindenberg was clearly visible in huge letters from the nose."*

Whilst this seemed to be a mercy errand, did it hide something more sinister?

## Spying Flights?

It was suspected at the time that these flights were spying flights to assess industrial sites across Northern England. Subsequent archive records show that there were indeed three ranking Nazi officers on board before the war as regular crew. These were Herbert Lau (Helmsman a Second Lieutenant in the SS, Rudolph Sauter  (Chief Engineer) and Walter Ziegler (Watch Officer)

Hindenberg Eye?

Archive records also show the existence of a Leica camera known as the Hindenberg Eye in the rear tailplane of the airship. The Telegraph and Argus of 20th November 2002 reported "*After the war photographs, probably taken from the airship, were discovered amongst German intelligence files of industrial sites, reservoirs and hospitals in the Skipton area, including Steeton bus depot, which could have been used as military installations and transport points.*"

The Yorkshire Evening Post reported in 1936 "*As far as aerial reconnaissance of industrial England is concerned it is there for the taking by the Hindenberg. We are simply making a gift of it. And what better way of observing our industrial layout is there than from the air.*"

### Local Photographs

Two local amateur photographers managed to take photographs of the Hindenberg as it flew over the area. The first managed on May 23rd to take a hurried photograph of the airship as it passed over Woodbank, Harden, and the second, Alfred Mitchell

*The Hindenburgh over Woodbank, Harden*

133

the Engineer at Bingley Teacher Training College took a rare shot of the Hindenberg flying over the College on 30th June 1936.

*The Hindenbergh above Bingley College*

## Hitlers HQ?

From a local point of view an article in the Bingley Guardian of 9th September 1977 stated *"records show that Hitler thought Bingley College might make a good local HQ for his occupation troops."*

Similar comment was made in the Leeds press in 1936 re the Hindenberg flying over the newly built Quarry Hill Flats. In May 2004, The Yorkshire Post under the Heading **'Don't dismiss stories of 'Hitler's HQ'** published several letters from readers who stated that relatives had first- hand knowledge or tangible evidence of Hitlers intentions. One of these also claimed that she had also watched two credible television programmes which supported the story.

Were these the reasons for the airships strange and what the local press called "interesting" flight path over the Aire Valley and Leeds? Was Bingley College indeed going to be considered as an invasion HQ?

Or where these just early examples of urban myth?

Unfortunately the Hindenberg was destroyed the following year when it caught fire and exploded whilst coming in to its mooring at Lakehurst USA,with the tragic loss of 36 lives.

# The BBC in Bingley

This Chapter looks at the first broadcast of a famous BBC Quiz show in 1946 and the reasons why Bingley was chosen as the venue for that first broadcast.

This is particularly poignant as the location where the broadcast was actually recorded was demolished in 2011 as part of the redevelopment of Beckfoot School, Bingley.

## Background to the Quiz Show itself

The recent Royal Wedding between Prince William and Kate Middleton managed to attract 24 million viewers to the BBC and ITV together. Can you imagine a weekly radio show which between 1946 and 1967 regularly pulled in 20 million listeners?

That show was called **Have a Go**, a quiz show which was hosted by **Wilfred Pickles** who was born in Halifax and was essentially the first BBC broadcaster to have a regional accent. At the time he was the biggest attraction on the radio and his show over the years would start with a piano played by amongst others, **Violet Carson** (later to star as Ena Sharples in Coronation Street) and the audience singing his signature tune "*Have a Go Joe*".

From the first show in March 1946 until 9th August 1946 the programme was aired on Home Services North under the title of Have a Go Joe. From 16th September 1946 until the last show in 1967 the programme was known as Have a Go and was broadcast on BBC Manchester for the Light Programme.

The show made Wilfred Pickles, his wife Mabel and **Barney Colehan** (one of a number of  Producers), household names who became nationally famous due to the catch-phrases used by Wilfred Pickles. These included:

- "*Ow Do, Ow are Yer?*" *(to contestants and the audience)*
- "*Are you courtin?*" *(to younger contestants)*
- "*What's on the table Mabel?*" *(a reference to local produce offered as additional prizes)*
- "*Give em the money Mabel*" *(or when Barney Colehan assisted) –* "*Give em the money Barney*".

Listeners were attracted to the show because it involved ordinary people who were encouraged to share intimate secrets or treasured memories in return for "having a go" at a quiz for which local produce and money prizes were offered.

Originally the prize money for the four questions asked was 2/6d (12.5p), 5 shillings (25p), 10 shillings (50p) and £1 which were awarded in increments up to a total of £1/17/6d (£1.87.5p) Wilfred and the show travelled nearly 400,000 miles over the 21 years that the programme was broadcast, presenting the shows once per week at factories, village and church halls, community centres, hospitals and other venues around the United Kingdom.

**Why was Bingley selected as the venue for the first ever broadcast?**

The reasons were that there were two significant coincidences:

In late 1945 **John Salt** the **great grandson of Titus Salt**, and who had been the BBC's North American Director, returned to the UK to take up the position of Northern Programme Director in Manchester. Salt contacted Wilfred Pickles and asked him if he would be interested in presenting a quiz show which involved ordinary people in answering simple questions for small cash prizes. The provisional working title for the show originally suggested was Quiz Bang (no doubt a play on words of the wartime phrase wizz bang referring to the sound made by a high velocity shell). This did not prove popular and Pickles suggested an alternative title, namely Have a Go Joe.

At a similar time the Editor of the **Bingley Guardian** newspaper Mr E B Gillespie challenged the **BBC** to organise a talent show in Bingley as he thought that there was much unrecognised talent locally.

As a result, the BBC contacted the Bingley Guardian expressing interest in organising the talent auditions and recording a new Quiz Programme idea from Bingley. Enquiries were made as regards booking the Princess Hall, Bingley but this was already booked and an alternative venue – **The Modern School** (now Beckfoot) was found. An advertisement in the Bingley Guardian on February 8th 1946 read:

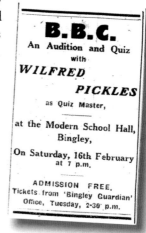

**B.B.C.**

An Audition and Quiz
with

*WILFRED*

*PICKLES*

as Quiz Master,

at the Modern School Hall,
Bingley,

On Saturday, 16th February
at 7 p.m.

ADMISSION FREE.
Tickets from 'Bingley Guardian'
Office, Tuesday, 2-30 p.m.

## The Recording on 16th February

In the event it was felt locally that perhaps the BBC had run the talent show auditions as a means of being able to attract a large audience and satisfy their primary aim of recording a new quiz show. Altogether, 1000 people attended the evening Audition and Quiz.

## The Talent Auditions

Private auditions were held in the afternoon and public auditions in the evening. As a result of these, the BBC Producer Philip Robinson promised to send details of Mabel Price a soprano of Bingley and Fred Richards a baritone from Baildon to the BBC Variety Producer for further consideration. Connie Baxter (piano) of Bingley was also highly commended and her details were forwarded to the BBC Music Department with a strong recommendation for a further audition.

## The Quiz

Ten volunteers took part in the Quiz with Corporal Peter Robinson (Bingley), William Ingham (Bingley), Geoffrey Chadwick (Eldwick), Joan Harding (Crossflatts) and Mrs Hallam (Bradford) successfully getting all four answers right and winning £1/17/6d each. Mrs Taylor (Bingley), Mrs A Baxter (Bingley), Wilfred Tetley (Bingley), Betty Wilkinson (Bingley) and Mrs Ellis (Bingley) contributed £1/15/0 shillings to the Jackpot by virtue of having got some answers wrong. This Jackpot was won by Geoffrey Chadwick who was the first to answer a mental arithmetic problem within the allocated thirty-seconds.

## Memorable Moments

Wilfred Pickles and contestants

According to *A Dictionary of Catch Phrases – British and American* (1992) Wilfred Pickles used his favourite catch-phrase to introduce the first broadcast in his broadest Yorkshire accent with the words *"Good Evening Ladies and Gentlemen of Bingley "ow do"* and *"ow are yer?"* The Bingley Guardian records that the audience answer was *"Alright Wilf"* and that all the way through the show, Pickles actively encouraged audience responses and participation.

The Bingley Guardian also notes that one of the contestants, William Ingham, introduced himself to Wilfred Pickles as "Pauline Walker's Husband". Jack Bailey of Bingley informs me through Sheila Donaldson of Bingley Local History Society that after the war he was a

*Excerpt of an advert for Pauline Walkers business*

business colleague of William Ingham, for whom he had the greatest respect. William told Jack about the broadcast. William was married to Pauline Walker who was a milliner in Park Road. As her shop was quite successful and well known locally, many people did refer to William as Pauline Walker's husband. After Have a Go was broadcast there was a fair amount of teasing from Bingley people who claimed that he had introduced himself in that way just to get more publicity for his wife's shop!

**Bingley Guardian**

Another contestant Wilfred Tetley had some banter with Wilfred Pickles about sharing the same Christian name. He was an employee of the Bingley Guardian and mentioned this proudly and loudly during his introduction which ensured that the newspaper received indirect publicity that it had not anticipated (?) It may not be exactly what the BBC had expected either!

The newspaper reports of the event that I have researched all make specific comment about the relaxed nature of both Philip Robinson and Wilfred Pickles and their encouragement of the audience and contestants to enjoy the occasion to the full. This was to be one of the prime reasons for the success of Have a Go over the next 21 years. Precedent and history were surely being made in Bingley that February evening.

**The Broadcast on March 4th**

The Radio Times for the week of the broadcast stated:

Monday 4th March 1946

8.30 – 9.00 "Have a Go Joe

The Quiz visits Bingley, Quiz Master, Wilfred Pickles, Music by Jack Jordans Quiztet. Produced by Philip Robinson (BBC recording)

The original recording was cut so that the broadcast was exactly 30 minutes in length, to fit in with BBC scheduling. This meant that two of the lower scoring quiz contestants were not included in the final broadcast.

The Bingley Guardian of 8th March 1946 included an article under the headline Bingley Makes History:

*"History was made for Bingley on Monday evening (4th March) when following the visit of the BBC to the town on February 16th, the Quiz recorded on that occasion was heard "on air" from 8.30 to 9 o'clock on the Northern Home Service. It is the first time Bingley itself actually has been given a broadcast."*

It seems from newspaper reports in the national, Bradford and Keighley press that the BBC visit to and broadcast from Bingley was a resounding success for all concerned.

### The Legacy of the Bingley Broadcast

The claim by the Editor of the Bingley Guardian *"Now that we have been "on air," perhaps we can say the Guardian has been able to make Bingley WORLD NEWS!"* may have been rather over-zealous. His further statement *"Certainly, we can say that money could not have bought the publicity which the town has received through the BBC effort"* was much nearer the mark. It would also appear that the approach used by "Pauline Walker's Husband" may have been the right one after all!

What is certain is that Bingley as the first in a series of over 1000 broadcast locations of Have a Go by Wilfred Pickles, played an important part in setting the format and template for the success of the programme which was to follow.

Sadly, John Salt of the BBC whose vision for the show brought it from an idea, to a national favourite died on 26th December 1947 at the age of 42. Consequently he was never to realise the full impact of his contribution to the runaway success of the show over its 21 year existence.

*The original venue at Beckfoot School before demolition in 2011*

# And finally....

The final chapter to this book established links between Titus Salt (1800's), a BBC Radio show (1900's) and the demolition of a Bingley school hall in 2011.Such is the quirky nature of local history.

**Of such "moments" are history made... and there are more.**

Check out **www.bradfordhistory.co.uk** for more information and details for the next publication.

## Photographs on the front cover

- Bingley Main Street
- Market Hall Butter Cross and Stocks
- Bingley Old Main Street
- Five Rise Locks

## Back cover

- Bingley Main Street
- Druids Altar
- Bingley Parish Church
- Goit Stock Waterfall
- The Glen - Ocean Wave Switchback
- The Glen - Japanese Gardens

# Bibliography and References

## Books

Alexander J et al (1997) *Benjamin Disraeli Letters 1852-1856*

Blake R (1966) *Disraeli*

Bonsai Society (1910) *The State of Horticulture in Britain, With an Eye to Japanese Gardening in the 1890's*

Briggs A (1960) *Chartist Studies*

Burrows D (1985) *Baildon – A Look at the Past*

Burrows D (1985) *Baildon – A Look at the Past*

Burrows D (1985) *Saltaire – A Look at the Past*

Burrows D (1985) *Saltaire – A Look at the Past*

Campbell M (2001) *In The Strange World of the Brontes*

Clarke R (2011) *A Penny for Going – A History of Saltaire and its regeneration told through its shops*

Cudworth W (1876) *Round About Bradford*

Disraeli B (1845) *Sybil*

Dodd E E (1930) *A History of the Bingley Grammar School*

Dodd E E (1958) *Bingley*

Downsborough E (2009) *The Lost Pubs of Bingley*

Firth G (1977) *Bingley History Trail*

Firth G and Hitt M *Bingley Past and Present*

Firth G (1999) *The Leeds and Liverpool Canal in Yorkshire*

Harrison W (1997) *Day's Awake – Childhood Memories of Bingley*

Hartley W (1900) *Fifty Years of Co-operation in Bingley : A Jubilee Record of the Bingley Industrial Co-operative Society, Ltd*

Horsfall Turner J (1897) *Ancient Bingley: Or Bingley, Its History and Scenery*

Kent A (1993) *What's That Chimney up There?*

Lawson P W G (1985) *The Bradford Antiquary Volume 1, Third Series*

Leach P and Pevsner N (2009) *The Buildings of England –West Yorkshire*

Leake M (2003) *In 100 Years at Shipley Glen – The Story of the Glen Tramway*

Matthews J, et al (1989) *Benjamin Disraeli Letters 1842-1847*

Mills H and Baldwin H (1995) *Images of England - Bingley*

Partridge E (1992) *A Dictionary of Catch Phrases – British and American*

Recks R J (1983) *Who's Who of Ballooning*

Roberts D (1979) *Paternalism in Early Victorian England*

H Speight (1898) *Chronicles and Stories of Old Bingley*

Taylor N and Symondson A (Architectural Review July 1968) *Burges and Morris at Bingley – A Discovery*

Van den Daele R and David Beale R - *Milner Field - The Lost Country House of Titus Salt Jr*

Varo S (1980) *Shipley Glen Ramble*

Ward J (2002) W B Ferrand – *The Working Man's Friend 1809 - 1889*

Wright D (1983) *The Chartist Risings in Bradford*

Wright L (1873) *In The Illustrated Book of Poultry*

## Public Papers

Bingley Conservation Area Assessment 2004)

Grade 2 Building Listing (1966)

Hansard (Volume 158) 14th June 1906

## Magazines and Journals

*Building News 15th March 1873*

*The Builder March 15th 1873*

*Yorkshire Journal (Issue 46-Autumn 2004) Deep in the Woods. Peter Smith*

## Brochure

*The Holy Trinity Church Centenary Brochure 1868 – 1968*

## Newspapers

Bingley Guardian Directory and Yearbook 1936

Bingley Guardian 8th February 1946

Bingley Guardian 8th March 1946

Bingley Guardian 9th September 1977

Bradford Observer 14th June 1869

Bradford Observer 21st June 1869

Bradford Observer 16th January 1873

Essex County Observer 9th June 1900

Glasgow Herald 10th June 1869

Hawera and Normanby Star (New Zealand) 27th August 1906

Huddersfield Chronicle 29th June 1895

Keighley News in May 1912

Keighley News 23rd April 1927

Leeds Intelligencer 8th April 1774

Leeds Mercury 15th November 1864

Leeds Mercury 28th May 1868

Leeds Mercury 10th June 1869

Leeds Mercury 5th March 1881

Leeds Mercury 27th December 1887

Leeds Mercury 6th March 1888

Leeds Mercury 31 June 1888

Leeds Mercury 18th March 1889

Leeds Mercury 12th March 1892

Leeds Mercury 6th August 1895

Liverpool Mercury 28th November 1823

Liverpool Mercury 11th September 1888

London Gazette 7th January 1868

Morning Chronicle 15th October 1844

New York Times 1st July 1906

Northern Echo 7th June 1848

Northern Star 10th June 1848

Pall Mall Gazette 25th September 1888

The Yorkshire Evening Post reported in 1936

Yorkshire Observer 1936

Yorkshire Post 25th May 2004 under the Heading *'Don't dismiss stories of 'Hitler's HQ'*